Contemporary Studies in Literature

Eugene Ehrlich, *Columbia University*

Daniel Murphy, *City University of New York*
Series Editors

Hermann Hesse

a collection of criticism edited by Judith Liebmann

McGRAW-HILL BOOK COMPANY
New York   St. Louis   San Francisco   Bogotá   Düsseldorf
Madrid   Mexico   Montreal   Panama   Paris   São Paulo
Tokyo   Toronto

123456789 MUMU 783210987

Library of Congress Cataloging in Publication Data

Main entry under title:

Hermann Hesse: a collection of criticism.

(Contemporary studies in literature) (McGraw-Hill paperbacks)
   Bibliography: p.
   1. Hesse, Hermann, 1877–1962—Criticism and inter-
pretation—Addresses, essays, lectures.   I. Leibmann,
Judith K.
PT2617.E85Z7215   838′.9′1209   77-3726
ISBN 0-07-037822-3 pbk.

Contents

Judith Liebmann

Introduction

When Hermann Hesse was awarded the Nobel Prize for literature in 1946, he was virtually unknown in the United States. Few of his novels had appeared in English translations here, and these, having been badly received, had gone out of print. Yet little more than twenty years later, Hesse had become the adored favorite of an entire generation of American youth. His books were selling by the millions, college seminars on Hesse sprouted up on almost every campus, and even rock groups were named after his heroes. The sudden and dramatic rise in Hesse's popularity left publishers and critics gasping for breath as they pursued the runaway market. Translations and paperback editions proliferated, while critical articles, new or reprinted, appeared in popular periodicals and serious journals. Much more than did the works themselves, it seemed, Hesse's fascination for American youth puzzled and occupied the critics, who saw his appeal less in any aesthetic or literary quality the works might possess than in the combination of social disenchantment, drugs, and Eastern religion to be found in them. A certain hippy ambience, the identity crises of his heroes, and Timothy Leary's adoption of Hesse as a literary mascot may all have lent impetus to the developing cult, but they surely cannot explain it.

Indeed, the recent Hesse wave in the United states was not a unique phenomenon. In 1958 Hesse appeared on the cover of *Der Spiegel* magazine, the German equivalent of *Time*, which used its own Newspeak in an attempt to explain the deep and long-lasting hold Hesse had maintained on Germany's post–World-War-II generation. Like American youths of the sixties, the young Germans of the late forties and fifties were disenchanted with the society and the world their elders had made for them and searched for alternatives within themselves or in new philosophies. *Der Spiegel*, like many American critics[1], suggested that

[1]See, for example, the review by Stephen Koch included in this volume.

1

Hesse's books and their appeal were based on the glorification of adolescent afflictions and that his audience was therefore limited to those in the throes of growing up. Whether ''youth'' is used as a pejorative or whether one recognizes the seriousness and creativity of the young and is willing to grant them credit in their choice of literary advocates, Hesse has always sparked a response among them. The enthusiasm in Germany and the United States since World War II was presaged by a still earlier period of youthful admiration. Thomas Mann, in his introduction to the English edition of *Demian*, recalls the effects of that early novel, published in 1919 under the pseudonym of Emil Sinclair:

> The electrifying influence exercised on a whole generation just after the First World War by *Demian*, from the pen of a certain mysterious Sinclair, is unforgettable. With uncanny accuracy this poetic work struck the nerve of the times and called forth grateful rapture from a whole youthful generation who believed that an interpreter of their innermost life had risen from their own midst—whereas it was a man already forty-two years old who gave them what they sought.[2]

That Hesse was already middle-aged when he wrote *Demian* and considerably older when he wrote such books as *Steppenwolf* and *Narcissus and Goldmund* underlines the fact that Hesse's concerns throughout his life and career remained centered on the questions of self-identity, self-awareness, and the conflict between the individual and society. Upon rereading *Narcissus and Goldmund* for the first time after more than twenty years, Hesse himself notes the recurrence of thematic material and the similarity of the heroes who embody it:

> It struck me again most forcibly that most of my longer works of fiction do not, as I believed during their writing, present new problems and portraits of new people in the way the true masters do but only repeat variations of the few problems and types congenial to me, though at new stages of life and experience . . . . But this insight did not pain me, . . . it meant something good and positive as well, it showed me that in spite of many ambitious wishes and efforts, on the whole I had remained true to my nature and had not abandoned the path of self-realization even at times of crisis and constraint.[3]

As he implies in this passage, the struggle for self-awareness and self-fulfillment characterized not only his fiction but his own life as well.

[2]*Demian*, trans. M. Roloff and M. Lebeck (New York: Harper and Row, 1965),pp. ix–x

[3]H. Hesse, *Autobiographical Writings,* trans. Denver Lindley (New York: Farrar, Straus & Giroux, 1972), p. 288.

His conflicts with family and society and the inner battles he fought within himself are of a piece with those of his heroes, from Knulp to Joseph Knecht. Born in 1877 in Calw, Württemberg, into a family of Protestant missionaries and expected to follow a similar path, Hesse caused both consternation and disappointment by giving up the study of theology and becoming instead an apprentice bookseller with literary ambitions. His writing brought him early success, however, with the publication in 1904 of his novel *Peter Camenzind*. Fame and, more important, a regular if modest income, enabled him to fulfill a dream he had of a ''farmer's idyll,'' the writer as *Bürger* surrounded by his family, living in peace and propriety. He moved with his bride, Maria Bernoulli, into a farmhouse in Gaienhofen on Lake Constance. The years in Gaienhofen were prolific, both for his family, which increased by three sons, and for his work, which included along with numerous contributions to journals and many lectures the novels *Gertrude, Beneath the Wheel,* and *Rosshalde.* Nevertheless, Hesse became increasingly dissatisfied with his life. The conflicts that arose in him between the ''man of imagination'' and the down-to-earth *Bürger* became increasingly disruptive. In 1912 he moved to Berne in hopes of alleviating the tensions and doubts that beset him more and more. Things continued to worsen, however. It was during these same years that Hesse experienced his first bitter encounter with the fickleness of an admiring public. Hesse was appalled by the nationalistic excesses and warmongering in Germany before World War I, and he wrote frequent and impassioned pacifist essays and letters denouncing them.[4] This antagonized friends and strangers alike, who reviled him publicly as a traitor.

The pressures, both external and internal, became unbearable in 1916, when his father died, his eldest son lay critically ill for more than a year, and his wife suffered a nervous breakdown that led to her confinement in an institution. At the edge of despair, Hesse entered into a long Jungian analysis that was to mark a turning point in his personal and literary life. Until then, Hesse's attempts to find harmony within himself between the imaginative life and the life of the bourgeois had been complicated and muddled by an overlay of moral and ethical questions that nagged at him. The psychological insights his analysis brought freed him from these considerations, at least to an extent that permitted him to pursue his own life more freely as he chose. They also provided the basis for a new approach to his writing. The romantic tone of his early fiction, the flowery prose and vague emotions, gave way to a more hard-edged, more experimental, more original style. The Freudian symbolism of

[4]Some of these are collected in the volume *If the War Goes On . . .* (New York: Farrar, Straus & Giroux, 1971).

Demian, the cool classicism of *Siddhartha*, and the great experiments of *Steppenwolf* mark Hesse's development into a modern writer, one whom Thomas Mann could compare to James Joyce and André Gide.[5]

In 1919 Hesse left his family in Berne to start a new life. Alone, he moved to the Swiss village of Montagnola, in the Ticino above Lake Lugano. In this remote spot he was able to take stock of himself and his life and devote himself with new vigor to his writing. Here he was to remain, with occasional trips to Germany or to the mountains, until his death forty-three years later. Almost immediately he wrote and published, at first and only briefly under the pseudonym Emil Sinclair, the novel *Demian*. Once again, as he termed it, he ''was on people's tongues.'' But Hesse remained in Montagnola, withdrawn both physically and emotionally from the turbulence of public renown, but writing assiduously. In the small apartment he occupied in the Casa Camuzzi between 1919 and 1931, Hesse wrote, among other works, *Kingsor's Last Summer*, *Siddhartha*, *Guest at the Spa*, *Journey to Nuremberg*, *Steppenwolf*, and *Narcissus and Goldmund*. In 1931, Hesse married Ninon Dolbin, with whom he moved into a new house in Montagnola, built for him as life tenant by his friend Hans Bodmer. During the thirties, Hesse's personal life approached the harmony he had been striving for so long. He wrote *Journey to the East* in 1932 and worked a decade on his last great novel, *The Glass Bead Game*, published in 1943. During these productive and happy years, Hesse grew increasingly disturbed by developments in Germany, but this time his political efforts were mostly confined to reviewing books by German writers, particularly those such as Broch or Kafka who were banned by the Nazis. Once again he found himself the object of scorn and derision from his native country, though his own works were not banned until 1943.

After the war, Hesse remained as aloof to his increasing popularity as he had been to his neglect, and he grew impatient with the many visitors who sought him out in Montagnola. He wished to maintain the serenity he had finally found, to write, to tend his garden, and to carry on an enormous correspondence, both with famous admirers, such as Thomas Mann, André Gide, and Romain Rolland, and with the scores of young people who continued until his death in 1962 to write long and fervid letters.

Until he was awarded the Nobel Prize for literature in 1946, the critical attention Hesse received was mostly a reaction to the political stands he either did or did not take. Even after this international recognition, he was celebrated as a ''German'' writer whose literary achievements were often given less attention than the fact that he was free of the

[5]Op. cit., p. ix.

Nazi taint and therefore able to serve as an inspiration to the postwar literary generation. Enthusiastic introductions to Hesse's works by Thomas Mann and André Gide are the best-known examples of this sort of praise.[6]

Beginning in the 1950s, particularly in the United States, Hesse became the subject of more serious, academically oriented and analytical critical scrutiny. The essays in the present volume have been chosen to reflect the scope of two decades of critical work and the direction it has taken. The first group of articles sees the works in the context of their cultural background, from a psychological, biographical, and literary point of view. In his classic analysis of the "metaphysical anxiety" that he sees as the driving force behind Hesse's work, Professor Seidlin emphasizes the existential and psychological (Jungian rather than Freudian) aspects that make Hesse a truly "modern" writer.

Professor Mileck, a major Hesse scholar and bibliographer, approaches Hesse's work from a biographical point of view combined with careful readings of the texts. He follows the development of Hesse's art, which he sees finally as egocentric, "confessional in form and therapeutic in function."

The article by Professor Freedman represents another milestone in Hesse criticism by placing him in literary perspective and showing the romantic elements in Hesse's work in their modern context.

The group of essays that follows these broad studies focuses on the works themselves, examining their aesthetic, stylistic, and structural elements. The late Professor Peppard's use of Hesse's story, "Edmund," as a key to his narrative techiques, Shaw's structural analysis of Siddhartha and its relationship to Buddhism, Ziolkowski's sensitive and original view of Steppenwolf, and Andrews' discussion of Hesse's poetry each show the insights that can be gained from careful and inspired modern textual criticism. Included in this group is the essay by Stephen Koch, which provides an example of the negative backlash, particularly among nonacademic critics, to Hesse's popularity.

The last articles emphasize the ideological aspects of Hesse's work and their social significance. Professor Heller examines Hesse's political, philosophical, and ideological views and the ways they are reflected throughout his career as an artist. The last essay, Timpe's review of Hesse's reception and rise to popularity in the United States, serves at the same time as a *caveat* not to allow the popularity of Hesse's ideas to overshadow the artistic and aesthetic achievements or the meanings of the works themselves.

[6]See André Gide's preface to *The Journey to the East,* reprinted in Ziolkowski, *Hesse: A Collection of Critical Essays* (Englewood Cliffs, N.J.: Prentice-Hall, 1973), pp. 21-24, and Thomas Mann's introduction, cited above.

The present volume, appearing as it does in the centenary of Hesse's birth, attempts to emphasize the enduring aesthetic and literary qualities of Hesse's works. The critical approaches represented here, though varied, are primarily concerned with questions of theme, structure, craftsmanship, and style and with more general areas of meaning and critical judgment. It is hoped that together they offer the modern reader of Hermann Hesse easier access to the beauty and mystery that have held the imagination of so many—and an admonition to maintain a critical gaze throughout the study of this fascinating writer.

Oskar Seidlin

Hermann Hesse: The Exorcism of the Demon

The conferring of the literary Nobel Prize for 1946 upon Hermann Hesse has brought into the international limelight, however briefly, a figure whose features were unfamiliar to the literary world at large. It has also illuminated the perplexing fact that our notions of literary greatness and fame are both arbitrary and relative in that an author, whose merits and standing are solidly confirmed at home, may be found "obscure" by foreign literary critics. The question that was being asked somewhat mockingly, "Who, after all, *is* Hermann Hesse?" must be disquieting to anybody familiar with contemporary German literature. And the fact that second and third rate German novelists and biographers gained easy admittance into our country, while only a few of Hesse's books were translated (and are now being gradually reissued), sets one thinking about the strange selective process at work in the establishment of a world literature. This phenomenon would lose its awkwardness if Hesse's talent, themes and problems were such as to appeal primarily to a narrowly defined home audience. But this is not the case. One cannot easily dismiss the fact that two such discerning and different writers as Franz Kafka and André Gide have counted Hesse among their favorites, while a true citizen of the world, Romain Rolland, has not only found him worthy of personal friendship but considered him one of his most interesting literary contemporaries. This, and the adoration which Hesse's *Demian* (published anonymously in 1919) enjoyed among the élite of German youth who clasped this book as if it embodied a new Revelation emerging from the apocalypse of the World War, may justify a closer analysis of Hermann Hesse's literary work. This evaluation will not deal with the obvious ties connecting Hesse with the poets of German Romanticism; it will not focus upon the socio-political concerns as expressed in his pacifist manifestos published during the First World War. Rather it will

Reprinted from Symposium, *vol. 4 (1950) by permission of the publisher.*

concentrate on Hesse's ruthless and self-tormenting exposure of the *condition humaine*, his metaphysical anxiety, that struggle with the demon and yearning for redemption which make him both a "modern" in the truest sense of the word and an ally of those who, by self-dissection, have made us painfully aware of the fate of man under the Sign of the Crisis.

I. AWAKENING

"In the beginning was the myth"—these are the opening words of Hesse's *Peter Camenzind* (1904), the novel which carried an almost completely unknown author to fame: rather incongruous opening words; for the story of the Swiss peasant lad who, after years of struggles, disappointments, self-deceptions and frustrating experiences in the literary world finally returns to his native village is much more closely related to the poetic realism of the late 19th century than to the myth-creating and myth-recreating efforts of our generation. Still, that these words introduce Hesse's first full-fledged literary achievement, that they stand as watchwords over his career, is no accident. The myth which is "in the beginning" will be forever the subsoil from which Hesse's works grow.

The myth is man's first answer to (or rather his first groping visualization of) the problems with which his own existence and his position in the cosmos confront him. It is man's awakening to himself, and it has all the landmarks of an awakening: the lingering on in the twilight region between night and day, the shock at the immediate directness of the new light, the courageous attempt to transpose experience of a primeval nature into the language and symbols of reality. In just this way Hesse's stories are myths; his entire work seems an endless recording of the process of awakening. The very word fascinates him, and in his last work, the monumental *Glass Bead Game* (1943), first published in this country under the title *Magister Ludi*, we find the protagonist's admission that "awakening was to me a truly magic word, demanding and pressing, consoling and promising." The process of waking in the morning was described with terrifying minuteness in *Kurgast* (*Guest at the Spa*, 1925), as memorable as the similar analysis in Proust's *Du côté de chez Swann*, but intensified by the horror of facing the light again, by the deadly desire not to venture across the threshold of a new day. A painful exercise in trespassing the threshold: this, and nothing else, is the essence of Hesse's works.

In the early novels, *Peter Camenzind* and *Beneath the Wheel* (1906), this "exercise" was still so much shrouded in psychological realism that Hesse appeared to be one more of the many sensitive and delicate anatomists of puberty. Hans Giebenrath, hero of *Beneath the Wheel*, falls all too clearly into the well-established type of the languid adolescent: troubles with an antagonistic father, endless conflicts with a cruel and impersonal school system, vague wanderings into the thoroughly bewildering realm of eros and sex, and finally the only half-intended suicide after some cheap carouse. Yet, in the light of Hesse's later development, it becomes quite obvious that the psycho-biological "case histories" of Peter Camenzind and Hans Giebenrath are only timid approaches to the painful process of awakening, timid even to the extent that both heroes shy away from passing through *la porte étroite*: Hans Giebenrath lets himself half-wittingly glide into the river, while Peter Camenzind returns to the quiet shelter of his home village where the "light of the day" does not penetrate. (The fact that in both cases the return to the dark is caused by failure to establish satisfactory sexual relations opens the door to psychoanalytic interpretations to which Hesse has been only too often subjected.) There is, in these early books, still a wall barring the adolescent hero from the open road, the same wall which separates young Hesse from the realization of his own inner self and of the problems which beset him and his time. A shock was needed to break down the barrier and bring an awakening which would force upon Hesse the reevaluation of all values, and open the road before him. The shock came in the form of the first World War.

From this time on, the veil which so strangely shrouded Hesse's earlier productions is ruthlessly drawn away. No longer does the poet shrink from taking the "forbidden fruit," from trespassing across the threshold between the stage of innocence and the acceptance of man's fate. No matter how painful this step might be, it has to be taken. In one of his short stories, "Klein and Wagner," written immediately after the War (1919), we read: "In reality there was only one thing which man feared: letting himself fall, taking the step out into the Unknown, the little step beyond all existing securities. But who has once, just once aban-doned himself, has just once given himself into the hands of fate, he is free." Klein, the hero of our story, has set himself free. After a secure life as a bank clerk he suddenly woke up and saw the humiliation caused by his daily routine, by marriage with a woman he had never loved and finally learned to hate, by the suppression of all noble and strong desires. This awakening was his "original sin": the little bank teller, before embarking on his road to freedom, defrauded his institution of a consider-able sum: he had fallen, but he was free. It would be hard not to see in this story, this little anecdote lifted from the everyday criminal register, a paraphrase of the story of the fall of man.

Protestant to the core, haunted by the consciousness of original sin, Hesse has circled again and again around man's tasting of the forbidden fruit of the tree of knowledge, his awakening amidst fear and trembling. The Forbidden which has to be faced exerts a dangerous but promising fascination. Already in *Beneath the Wheel* there was a dark and slimy alley which exuded "together with a strangely foul air a blissfully uncanny anguish, a mixture of curiosity, anxiety, bad conscience and heavenly premonitions of adventures." All of Hesse's heroes are simultaneously repelled and attracted by this dark alley, none more strongly than the young protagonist of "A Child's Soul" (1919), whose story becomes one of the most terrifying records of mental anguish in contemporary literature. Drawn to his father's room, where he has no business to be, he rummages in all the corners and drawers of the study "only to follow a compulsion which almost choked me, the compulsion to do evil, to hurt myself, to load myself with guilt." When the Serpent whispers, Adam will not resist, the sin has to be committed. And so the youngster in "A Child's Soul" steals fruit from his father's drawer, not an apple but a few dried figs (and that the fig tree is introduced makes the "mythical" impact of the story perhaps more obvious than necessary.)

The urge to find out the "secret" about one's self and the hidden corners of life, curiosity in the widest and most dangerous sense, is the driving force behind Hesse's work. It is a ruthless curiosity, shameless and without mercy, and it will not rest until the last veil is drawn back. For this reason then, and not for the sake of psychological subtleties, Hesse has delved again and again into the minds of vagrants and adolescents, since for them everything is unknown and without name before they have "found out." They are all spies tracking themselves down, excited by the scent of the Unknown, hankering after secrets. They are all very much akin to the Kierkegaard who admitted that it would have given him great satisfaction to be a member of the Copenhagen criminal police force. They are all brethren of Gide's protagonists, the ruthless exposers and explorers, the snoopers through *Les Caves du Vatican*, living embodiments of a curiosity which never seems to exhaust itself so that the very last sentence of *The Counterfeiters* can start with the words: "Now I am curious. . . ." In one of his early writings, a collection of fairy tales, short stories, diary pages and poems entitled *Hermann Lauscher* (1901), Hesse calls Lauscher's most characteristic feature a "self-tormenting love for truth," and he could have hardly found a more appropriate self-characterization. He is consumed by an uncontrollable and at times embarrassing desire to be naked, to show himself in so merciless a light that even the "private parts" of body and soul will not be spared exposure. In his story "Klingsor's Last Summer" (1919), the painter Klingsor gathers in his final hours the strength to do his self-portrait. And this is what his friends see when, after Klingsor's death, the picture has been found: "It is Man, Ecce Homo, the tired, rapacious, wild, child-like and overrefined man of our late period, homo Europaeus, dying and desiring to die: purified by every longing, sick with every vice, enthusiastically elated by the knowledge of his destruction, ready for every progress, ripe for each regression, all glow and all fatigue, devoted to fate and pain as the morphinist is to his drug, lonesome, hollowed out, old as the ages, at the same time Faust and Karamasov, animal and sage, all bare, without any ambitions, all naked, full of a child's fear of death and full of the weary readiness to die his death.'' It is Klingsor's portrait, but not Klingsor's alone. It might be Nietzsche's portrait, of Man on the Eve of the Superman—if it were not Hesse's portrait of Hesse. To find the same merciless exposure in the ''first person,'' one has only to leaf through the *Guest at the Spa*, the abysmal record of a sick man who, with masochistic satisfaction, watches the deformations, pains and ridiculous motions of his sciatica-ridden body.

But this violent urge for confession is mixed with a stubborn secretiveness, a bashful hiding behind the ''fig leaf,'' an obstructive silence opposed to the asking and demanding voice: ''Adam, where art Thou?'' Guilt cries out for confession, but guilt breeds a dark recalcitrance as well. In the first story of the Lauscher collection, written as early as 1896, we meet for the first time this bliss of confession mixed with the stubborn refusal to admit one's wrong which will shake the Steppenwolf no less than Emil Sinclair, hero of *Demian*. The conflict of remorseful desire to do penance and of rebellious self-assertion in the face of the power which demands submission is being incessantly fought on the battlefield of the soul, and vests Hesse's works with an urgency and tension truly religious. In the very signature which Hesse puts under his writings we can trace this bewildering spectacle of confession and hiding. Is it not revealing that one of his very first works presented itself to the audience as *The Posthumous Writings and Poems of Hermann Lauscher*, edited by Hermann Hesse; that his latest one is entitled *The Glass Bead Game, the Attempt of a Life Chronicle of Magister Ludi Joseph Knecht*, edited by Hermann Hesse; that his *Demian* appeared anonymously with the subtitle *The Story of Emil Sinclair's Youth*; that *Steppenwolf* (1927) pretends to be the autobiography of a certain Harry Haller, found in his room after he has mysteriously left the town where he lived for a few months? There is a permanent hiding behind pseudonyms, behind a mere editorship—in short: a recalcitrance to ''admit'' which is ironically counteracted by the urge to expose himself, to ''confess.'' Lauscher's first name is not Hermann by chance; the initials of the Steppenwolf are not incidentally H. H. (which, by the way, are the initials of the hero of *Journey to the East* [1932] as well), and for good reasons the first Magister Ludi, the inventor of the *Glass Bead Game*, is called Calwer, the man from Calw, the little town in Swabia where Hesse was born in 1877, and which with its old houses, narrow streets and murmuring brooks appears in almost all of Hesse's stories. These are more than playful attempts to mystify the reader. They are true symptoms of this bliss of confession mixed with the stubborn refusal to admit one's wrong. And it seems quite characteristic that Hesse has never called any of his books a ''novel'' but has rather chosen the noncommittal term a ''narrative,'' which leaves the question between ''confessional'' authenticity and ''impersonal'' fiction in an ambiguous balance.

II. FATHER AND MOTHER IMAGE

A balance? Rather an indication of the basic polarity which runs through all of Hesse's works. Except for the two ''narratives'' which present Harmony Regained, *Siddhartha* (1922) and *The Glass Bead Game*, it will be obvious even to the casual reader that each of Hesse's major books has a double focus, has two heroes which are ''two'' in the sense in which a schizophrenic is ''two'': in *Beneath the Wheel* Hans Giebenrath and Hermann Heilner; Narcissus and Goldmund; Demian as the Companion of Emil Sinclair, the narrator; and finally the Steppenwolf, who is equally two, if not many more, in one. This cleavage of personality symbolizes the two elements which constitute man and his world: the father element and the mother element. It is only during the war years that the metaphysical polarity of these two worlds finds its full and unambiguous expression in Hesse's work. While the mother, embodiment of all sensuous, vital and elemental principles, remained inconspicuous and pale in *Peter Camenzind*, she was totally absent in *Beneath the Wheel*. In *Rosshalde* (1914), the story of an artist's unhappy marriage, man and woman are pitted against each other, but they are seen from the ''wrong angle,'' as husband and wife rather than as father and mother. The war is still waged on the physical and psychological front; it is only after the ''awakening'' that it will be shifted to the mythical level, that father and mother will emerge as archetypes, as the embodiments of the spiritual and vital energies fighting in and for man.

In ''A Child's Soul'' the two worlds are seen as opposite polarities. ''Downstairs in our house mother and child were at home, a harmless air pervaded the place; but upstairs power and spirit were dwelling, here was tribunal and temple and the realm of the father.'' This Upstairs (we cannot help associating the structure of the Christian cosmos) ''smelled of sternness, of law, of responsibility, of father and God.'' The rule and suppression which the father-God imposes upon Hesse's heroes are responsible for the wild outbursts of rebellion with which his books, written in the late teens and early twenties, are swarming. No psychoanalyst is needed to diagnose the neuroses and violent traumas of the patients. Oedipus is at work in Emil Sinclair's frightful dream in which he sees himself hiding behind the trees, armed with a glittering knife which the seducer has put into his hands, ready to jump upon the tall figure walking down the alley: his ·father. Oedipus is at work in the blasphemous and delirious ravings of the youngster in "A Child's Soul," after the sin has been committed: "I have killed, I have burned down houses, because I had fun doing it and because I wanted to mock at you and rile you. See, I hate you, I spit at your feet, you God. You have tortured and flayed me, you have given laws which nobody can obey."

Even though these and similar quotations point strongly in the psychoanalytic direction, it would be wrong to tag Hesse too ostentatiously with the ever-handy Freudian label. Hesse's concern is a truly religious one, the groping and hoping for personal salvation, and Freud's secularization of God as a pure magnification of the individual father, his interpretation of the religious emotion as a disease symptom, would seem to Hesse no less unacceptable than it was to Kafka. It is characteristic enough that in the earlier works, in which the father-son conflict is at its highest pitch, the mother is totally or almost totally absent. It is only in *Demian* that "the mother" plays a decisive role in the development of the hero. Yet, her very name, Mrs. Eve, identifies her as the mythical All-Mother, the great womb in which all life rests—and not as the individual Freudian libido object. Those who have tried to fit Hesse to the Procrustean bed of Freudianism overlook the fact that Mrs. Eve is not "mother" but "mother image," not a psychophysical reality but a myth, clearly evidenced by the fact that she is not Sinclair's mother (who does not appear in the book at all), but the mother of Sinclair's "double," Demian. To be sure, she is sex object too (the gossip about the incestuous relations between her and her son Demian is revealing). But the emphasis lies on her relationship to and meaning for Sinclair, and in this relationship the Oedipus-Jocasta motif is entirely lacking. Sinclair's long and painful pilgrimage to the "mother" does not describe the process of emerging from a dark individual neurosis to the unmysterious and rational daylight, but rather a descent into the dark mysteries of the "Essence," into the procreativeness of motherly life. A Freudian interpretation would achieve here what it always achieves: the reduction of a symbolic image to its purely psychophysical elements and, by the very rationalistic process of this reduction, the destruction of the ontologic authenticity of the symbol. (It is not surprising that for many years Hesse was under treatment by a disciple of C. G. Jung, whose objection to Freud is mainly based on Freud's rationalistic destruction of the superindividual myth, and that *Demian* was written as part of his analysis.)

It is in *Steppenwolf* that the two elements clash most violently: man, the detached and cool evaluator of values, the rational and demanding lawgiver and judge locked in deadly battle with the animal, whose ambition it is to break all "civilized" fetters by the assault of his vital instincts, sneering triumphantly at the hopeless attempt to keep the mother world, the drives and desires of the amoral natural forces of life, in chains. This schizophrenic duel finds its most nightmarish expression in the double-taming scene which Harry Haller witnesses in the "magic theater," the place where his inner turmoil is externalized on an imaginary stage in a series of wild spectacles. In a merciless mirror, Harry Haller sees himself cracking the whip over the well-trained, emasculated wolf, until the wolf takes over and now, whip in his paws, forces Harry to walk on all fours, to debase himself to the lowest animal level.

These shrill and cacophonous tones, which remain unresolved in *Steppenwolf*, find their harmonious resolution in *Narcissus and Goldmund*. Clearer than ever before, father and mother principle, Spirit and Life, are confronted: Narcissus, abbot of the monastery, the thinker who lives in the self-sufficient loneliness of the intellect, and Goldmund, the young novice whose very name (Golden Mouth) indicates his hunger for life, the joyful exuberance of pouring himself into the stream of being. It is Goldmund's story which is being told, his tours and detours in search of the Great Mother. "Strange haunting dreams of delight and triumph, visions of her in whom all his senses had his share, and then, with its scents and longings, the mother world would be about him: its life calling enigmatically: his mother's eyes were deeper than the sea, eternal as the gardens of paradise. Life would taste sweet and salt upon her lips; his mother's silky hair would fall around him, tenderly brushing his mouth. And not only was this mother all purity, not only the skyey gentleness of love: in her, somewhere hidden between enticements, lay all the storms and darkness of the world, all greed, fear, sin and elemental grief, all birth, all human mortality." With these visions before his eyes, Goldmund breaks out of the cloister and starts upon his enraptured dance of love. An endless chain of sensuous and sexual experiences: the gypsy girl, the peasant's wife, the two high-born sisters, the servant maid, the Jewess Rebecca, the count's mistress. If Hesse avoids monotony in this merry-go-round of the senses, it is due to the fact with each new beloved Goldmund becomes a new lover. He is a true vagabond, a true explorer of the delights and ills of the mother world, an artist not only when he tries to carve in wood the faces and bodies he has loved, but also when he becomes one with them in flesh. His vagrancy is in truth an earnest and pious quest, his hunger for life does not taste of the nihilistic attempt to plunge headlong into life out of fear of death. In Klingsor's hectic vitality the panic of the "last summer" still reared its ugly grimace. His craving for burning and intoxicating colors was nothing but a running away from death already waiting at the gates. There is no panic in Goldmund's rovings. The Black Death, which hits the country while Goldmund's roaming is in its height, and which throws the world around him into a delirious frenzy of lust and greed, only helps Goldmund to strengthen his equilibrium and to withdraw into an idyll, one of the very few that the vagabond finds in his restless wanderings. Goldmund's pilgrimage is an act of self-realization, not of self-defense. His indulgence is not born out of the dogmatic, purposeful opposition of an anti-intellectual intellectual, as is the case in so many of D. H. Lawrence's writings with which *Narcissus and Goldmund* has been quite unjustifiably linked. *Lady Chatterley's Lover* is pornographic for the very reason that it represents a "gospel" (though it is the resentful gospel of an Anti-Christ) which, by its very opposition to the values it wishes devaluated, destroys the innocence of the flesh it strives to celebrate. Goldmund's exuberance is free of the corrosive gnawings of an anti-intellectual revelation; his devotion to the All-Mother is borne up by the all-embracing pantheism of a St. Francis of Assisi. (It is not without interest that very early in his career [1904] Hesse published a short monograph of the childlike saint whose exalted love for all beings flowed into the dithyrambic Song to the Sun.)

The violent tension of *Steppenwolf* is overcome. Father and mother worlds have ceased to be irreconcilable enemies. In *Narcissus and Goldmund* the two worlds are conceived from the outset as opposite yet complementary poles between which man's existence is suspended. No longer is the father the exacting and punishing authority set over life as a stern and hostile ruler. As a monk, and later abbot of the cloister, Narcissus is at the same time "father" and "brother" to the mother-child. From his face all the threatening and antagonistic features have vanished. Brooding in monastic loneliness over the timeless rules and patterns, he is the embodiment of the pure Spirit, remote from ever-changing life with its organic rhythm of birth, growth and decay. He is the *logos* which was "in the beginning" (it is not by chance that he is presented as a distinguished logician and mathematician), in him rests the dead eternity of the Spirit. But this father, "Father" Narcissus, is no longer hostile to life, to the world of fleeting phenomena. It is Narcissus who opens for Goldmund the door into life; it is he who takes him back to his heart after the lost son has spent strength and life in his search for the Mother. Goldmund was in his mind during all the years of separation, but he was no less in Goldmund's life during all the stages of the wild pilgrimage. For to Goldmund, the artist, who, in his creations, immortalizes the mortal moment, snatches lasting images from the ever-changing stream of life, the world of the father is always present. And it is highly fitting that, when Goldmund carves his first sculpture, the figure of St. John the Baptist, it is Narcissus' face which takes shape under his hands. In art the two poles, the world of the father and the world of the mother, seem to merge into a synthesis. And yet, a full and permanent union is impossible. The Matrix which is the chaos will always elude the grip of the *logos*. The supreme image, the statue of Eve, the All-Mother, which Goldmund has carried in his heart all his life, he will never be able to finish. Death, the world of the father, in which there is no growth, no form, no dream, where there is only the imageless stillness of the thought, will overcome Goldmund before the supreme achievement is even begun. But where, Narcissus, is your victory? The last words of Goldmund, ringing forever in the Father's ears long after the beloved vagabond has died in his arms, are a last and paradoxical defiance of the mother world: "But how will you ever die, Narcissus? You know no mother. How can we love without a mother? Without a mother, we cannot die." In this last scene in which Narcissus sees life slowly fade out of the eyes of his beloved one, there is a gleam of the Beatific Vision in which the word has become flesh and the flesh has become word.

III. THE GREAT EXORCISM

There is only a gleam of the Beatific Vision, and to achieve even that much, one has to "travel through the hell in myself," a phrase by which Hesse has summarized the substance of his *Demian*. And this phrase is the theme of all of Hesse's works, at least up to *Narcissus and Goldmund*. What is this hell in myself? It is the religious term for the conflicts arising from man's divided nature, for the chaos of chthonic, inchoate forces in us which, as long as they are not integrated in a controlled and controllable order, exert a subterranean but no less tormenting tyranny over us. In the exposition of this chaos and of the anxiety which it breeds in us, Hesse has been untiring. *In Sight of Chaos* he called a series of essays on Dostoevsky (1919), whom he has rightly considered his closest fellow traveler into the abyss of the human soul, and "in sight of chaos" might well be the general title of all his works from *Rosshalde* to *Steppenwolf*. No Freud was needed to open his eyes to the "dark aspects of the soul"; he has learned from the "original" masters, the German Romanticists, Dostoevsky, Nietzsche. At the age of 23 he wrote in his diary (later included in his *Hermann Lauscher*): "At that point I began to feel that the hour of a long-postponed battle had inexorably come, that everything suppressed, chained, half-tamed in me was tearing at the fetters, exasperately and threateningly. All the important moments of my life in which I had deprived the feeling of the Eternal, the naïve instincts, the innate unconscious life of some of their territory, gathered before my memory like an enormous, hostile host. Before their onslaught all thrones and columns trembled. And now I knew suddenly that nothing could be rescued. Unloosened, the lower world in me was reeling forth, it broke and sneered at the white temples and favorite images. And still I felt these desperate rebels and iconoclasts related to me, they wore the features of my dearest memories and childhood days.''

It is this division in us that is the source of all our anxieties. ''And why are they frightened?'' asks Demian. ''One is frightened when one is not in self-agreement. They fear because they have never said 'yes' to themselves. A community of human beings who are afraid of the Unknown in them.'' To cure the disease no shortcut is available. The first therapeutic step is to decompose by relentless probing the easy securities which tend to divert our attention from the schism which rages in us. The first duty is the confession of the disease, the almost proud admission that we are psychopathics. Such was the courage of Dostoevsky: he was a prophet, a messenger of a higher and truer life because he was a hysteric and epileptic (*The Brothers Karamasov or the Decline of Europe*); such was the courage of Nietzsche who had dared to ask the ''terrible and harassing question whether under certain historic and cultural conditions it was not worthier, nobler and more proper to become psychopathic than to adjust oneself to these conditions by sacrificing one's ideals'' (*Guest at the Spa*). This, so Hesse continues at this point, ''has been the topic of almost all of my writings.'' It has indeed. And it was this very courage to ''become psychopathic'' which, in the eyes of postwar German youth, raised his *Demian* to the level of a revelation. Here was a man who, after all the false securities had broken down, did not offer them a new program by which to adjust themselves, by which to join quickly the broken pieces into a new but certainly not firmer structure. Here was a man who showed them that there was only one thing left: to be glad that all the deceptive supports and props had gone, that the road was clear now for the investigation of the disease and for its possible cure. The message that resounded from *Demian* echoed forth even more strongly from Hesse's philosophical essay *Zarathustra's Return* (1920). It was Nietzsche's message, but already the literary presentation—the sage walking with his disciples at the outskirts of the town, provoking questions and answering them—made it clear that it was another philosopher's message as well: Socrates' message: Know Thyself.

To know oneself, to explore the hidden corners in one's soul, not to flinch even if one finds these corners populated with beasts and demons, this is the purpose of Emil Sinclair's, Steppenwolf's, Goldmund's travels. These descents into the subconscious, into the lower world, may, at times, read like samples from a psychoanalyst's handbook; but again, the direction of Hesse's genius was established long before he was ever exposed to Freud. It is the following program which, in 1900, Hesse outlines in "Lauscher's" diary: "To lift everything to the surface, to treat oneself to everything Unspoken and Unspeakable as to an unveiled mystery!" And not knowing Freud yet, he continues characteristically enough: "I know very well, this is Romanticism." If *Demian* and *Steppenwolf* are applied Freudianism (we have made our qualifications above), they are at least as closely related to the great "midwifery" of Socratic dialogues; they are records of a merciless exorcism and conquest of the dark powers which we have "to lift to the surface" in order to know ourselves. It is Narcissus who quite consciously formulates the principle of midwifery: "Some demon must be at work in Goldmund, a hidden fiend to whom it was permitted to divide this noble being against itself . . . . Good then, this demon must be named, exorcised and made visible to all and, when this was done, he could be conquered."

As every patient has his analyst, so every one of Hesse's travelers on "The Way Within" (under this title Hesse collected a number of his shorter stories) has his midwife Socrates: Hans Giebenrath his Hermann Heilner, Emil Sinclair his Demian, Goldmund his Narcissus, the Steppenwolf a whole group of them: the mysterious author of the inserted "Treatise Concerning the Steppenwolf," the girl Hermine who is only a female materialization of his schoolmate Hermann, and the strange musician who is Pablo and Mozart in one. They are all externalizations of the inner teacher who leads the hero on his way; and that the name "Demian" resembles in sound so closely to "daimon," the voice which, according to Socrates, guides and awakens the soul of the disciple, is certainly not accidental. (It may be mentioned in parenthesis that the name of the hero of *Demian*, Emil Sinclair, equally evokes in the German reader the association with Greece. Sinclair was the closest friend of Germany's most exalted and tragic spiritual traveler to Greece, Friedrich Holderlin, whose main work, *Hyperion*, represents the most magnificent transplantation of the Greek *paidaia* unto German soil.) What these "midwives" impart to their disciples is the "viper bite of philosophy" of which Alcibiades speaks in his eulogy to Socrates, this festering sting driving to self-realization. It is the supreme and most subtle form of seduction because it does not quench the thirst but heightens it, the thirst and longing to know oneself. And when Sinclair calls his friend Demian a "seducer," he is a clairvoyant as were the archons of the city of Athens who condemned Socrates to death for seduction of the youth. For he who has learned to know himself will no longer bow to the lures and threats of authority. He has become free.

On this road to freedom travels Emil Sinclair, driven on by Demian's voice, the permanent and catalytic mobilizer of "anamnesis," although here we are not faced with the remembering of innate "ideas" but with the rediscovery of all the emotional and vital urges which are lurking underneath the surface and have not yet become "members" in the chain of Sinclair's being. "You know that 'your permitted world' was only half of the world, and you have tried to suppress the other half as the priests and teachers are doing"—this is Demian's "viper bite of philosophy," and it tears open the wound through which Sinclair's lower world will tumble into the light of day: a series of dreams, drawings and paintings welling up from the unconscious, haunting reminiscenses of images which he has seen in his childhood. And there will always be Demian or one of his mysterious messengers who will interpret these symbols for him, will throw open the door to a world which "the priests and teachers" laboriously try to camouflage, until Sinclair finally reaches Mrs. Eve, the source of all life, until he finds and learns to know—himself.

It is in much wilder and dissolute stages that the Steppenwolf is exorcised. Already the composition of the book makes it plain that we are again on "The Way Within." The first observation point is still far outside: the anonymous young man in whose house the Steppenwolf used to live and with whom he had an occasional talk. The second step brings us closer: the Steppenwolf's diary, by which Harry Haller introduces himself, has been found. The third step takes us inside: it is the inserted "Treatise Concerning the Steppenwolf" ("For Madmen Only"), a mercilessly rational exposition of the "case" drawn up by a mysterious, completely detached observer. The fourth step: Harry Haller's life as the concrete presentation of the problems which the Treatise has analyzed theoretically, and finally, the fifth step, the initiation into the "magic theatre" where the pandemonium of his soul materializes itself before his eyes in a series of Punch-and-Judy shows. It is a boring beneath the surface until at the end the hidden demons appear in a frightening and unbridled mummery. So complete and ruthless is the unmasking of the subconscious powers and drives that a realistic frame, which still existed in *Demian* , can no longer accommodate them. Only a "magic theater," working with all the ghoulish tricks of a Grand Guignol, can furnish the proper stage for this supreme exorcism.

However, the heightened frenzy of this raising of the demons does not only indicate that the schism between the two worlds has become deeper and more dangerous; it points toward a much more serious affliction: the raging against the principle of "personality," of individuation as such. Emil Sinclair was groping for the road to himself, for self-encounter which would lead to self-realization and freedom for himself. What Harry Haller is after is freedom from himself, the complete destruction of the bond which holds the particles of the Ego together and establishes the unity of the person. It is an "analysis" whose aim is no longer integration but utter dissolution of the Ego. Harry Haller does not suffer from a "split" personality, but from the individuation of man in personality as such. The "Treatise Concerning the Steppenwolf" describes the situation aptly: "The body is always one, but of the souls that live in it, there are not two or five, but innumerable ones. Man is an onion consisting of hundreds of layers . . . . The old Asiatics realized and knew it very well, and in the Buddhist yoga they invented an exact technique for unmasking the delusion of personality." Harry Haller is afraid of self-encounter (again and again suicide seems to him the only possibility of deliverance), his descent into the hell is not guided by the demand for remembering, but by the desire for complete dismembering. His watchword is no longer "find yourself," but "dissolve yourself into nothingness"; his exorcism is yoga. It is only at the end of the self-annihilating magic-theatrical performance, which Haller watches with the masochistic desire to punish himself for his individuation, that he is called to order by Mozart: "Of course, you'd fall for every stupid and humorless arrangement, generous gentleman that you are, for anything full of bathos and devoid of wit. Well, I shan't fall for it, I won't give you a nickel for your whole romantic penitence. You want to be beheaded, you want to have your head chopped off, you madman. For this idiotic ideal you might commit another ten murders. You want to die, coward that you are, but not live. But in the devil's name: live—that's just what you are to do." The road into the interior, which threatened to become a road into nothingness and dissolution, has led once more to the self. The mirrors of the magic theater, which might have refracted the rays of the personality into infinity, have merged into a lens where the beams are gathered again in a cone. Analysis has resulted in "Gestalt," the unleashing of the demons in a conquest over them. At the end of the exorcism the door of the magic theater leads into the open and Harry Haller knows: "Mozart is waiting for me."

IV. INDIVIDUATION, TIME AND IRONY

It is in *Steppenwolf*, which again and again has been proclaimed as plainly "psychoanalytic," that the decisive difference between Hesse and Freud becomes apparent. What Freud tries to repair is the disturbance of man's functional existence in the world; the malady which Hesse exposes time and again is the disturbance of man's authenticity, his *Eigentlichkeit*, as Heidegger puts it. Freud is a reformer who points at curable diseases, Hesse is an existentialist who points at the malaise inherent in the *condition humaine*.

Before Harry Haller enters the magic theater, his psychogogue Pablo (who will later appear as Mozart) opens his eyes to the real root of his sufferings: "Undoubtedly you have guessed long ago that the conquest over time, the deliverance from reality is nothing else but the desire to get rid of your so-called personality. This is the jail in which you are sitting." The true (and incurable) plight of man began with his individuation, with his separation from the All-ness, with the beginning of time. Time is the horrible proof that paradise is lost, that man is no longer living in his *Eigentlichkeit*, but in the all-powerful and tormenting sequence of moments (this is what Heidegger calls *die Geworfenheit*), the permanent transcience of all things and of his own existence. It is man's curse that he can no longer live in the simultaneousness of his experience, that he is suspended between eternity which knows only past and future, and time which knows only the transitory moment. Now it becomes evident that the great exorcism which we tried to analyze above means more than the schism in the individual soul: it is the paradoxical attempt to mobilize all the powers, actions and reactions of the soul into an ever-present simultaneity (Heidegger calls it *Zuhandenheit*) which will be capable of outwitting the deadening course of time. Klingsor's desperate cry, "Why does time exist? Why always only this idiotic one-after-the-other and never an effervescent, satiating at-the-same-time?" rings through all of Hesse's writings up to the *Glass Bead Game*. If one could keep the moment alive, if one could rescue all one's yesterdays, then the suffering would be gone. And in this attempt to conquer time, Hesse's heroes are the true companions of Proust's, Joyce's, Thomas Mann's protagonists. They are all *á la recherche du temps perdu* (although their tensions and their revolts against the "idiotic" one-after-the-other are much more violent then Proust's and much more akin to James Joyce's); they are all in the process of a remembrance of things past (which, however, is a suitable title for Proust's *oeuvre* only when the word "remembrance" is taken in the special sense suggested here.)

But how is the eternalization of the moment possible? Hesse does not attempt to give an answer to the unanswerable question. In none of his "solutions" is finality. But in every single one of his books there is the attempt to face the insoluble bravely and honestly. There are the attempts of the "artists," of Klingsor and Goldmund, who give themselves to the moment so unreservedly in the hope that the very intensity of living will save it from destruction. But in the case of Klingsor the insatiability is nothing but an outgrowth of the *horror vacui*, and Goldmund must realize that his life is spent before the ultimate task, the sculpture of Lady Eve, can take shape. Still, art seems to hold a promise, it might become the powerful weapon which can defeat the dance of death. And Goldmund ponders: "When as craftsmen we carve images or see laws to formulate our thoughts, we do it all to save what little we may from the linked, never ending dance of death." In music, above all, the solution seems to be reached. In the *Steppenwolf*, and particularly in *The Glass Bead Game*, music appears as deliverance from the curse of the one-after-the-other. On one of the mysterious streamers over the different showcases in the magic theater, Harry Haller reads the inscription: "The Essence of Art. The Transformation of Time into Space through Music." And even before he entered the magic theater, he had come to the realization: "Yes, that was it, this music was something like time frozen to space and above it hovered a superhuman serenity, an eternal, divine laughter." To "live in music"—that might be the answer, to develop in time but not to be subject to the law of succession and transiency, to transcend each moment by fitting it into a timeless harmony, in short, to live in humor. "To live in the world as if it were not the world, to respect the law and yet to stand above it, to possess as if one did not possess, to renounce as if it were no renunciation, all this only humor is capable of achieving." (*Steppenwolf*.) It means what one might call to live symbolically, to be in the things but to be beyond them at the same time, to analyze while experiencing and to experience while analyzing. It is exactly what Thomas Mann has defined again and again as the attitude of irony. It is, in terms of Heidegger's Existentialism, the permanent blending of *Geworfenheit* with *Vorlaufen zum Tode*. In his *Guest at the Spa*, Hesse has given, with the help of a clinical case, an example of how the ironic solution can lift us beyond the tormenting pressure of the "moment," of the cage in which we sit. By living in irony, by living as if he were playing a role which he can watch and analyze as an outsider, the sciatica-ridden guest of the health resort has cured himself, perhaps not from the disease of his swollen and creaking joints, but from the much deeper disease which made the physical illness unbearable. One day, after having dragged for many weeks his painful limb through the deadly monotony and the dead-earnest healing routine of the sanatorium, he lifts himself above his miserable existence and looks at himself from the outside. And seeing a ridiculous hypochondriac, worried about every motion that might cause him pain, shuffling down the staircase, putting the chair in the right angle so that sitting down will become easier, he bursts out into laughter which opens the road to recovery. It is the salvation through irony, the annihilation of the moment by transcending its laws and conditions, it is the being oneself and not being oneself at the same time which, on the intellectual level, is expressed in the patient's ironic statement: "I have the misfortune that I always contradict myself."

It is the very attitude which Kierkegaard scorned in his "Either-Or" as the "aesthetic" one because it lacks the absoluteness, the firm conviction that time and eternity are irreconcilable antipodes, that we cannot save ourselves under any circumstances. It is man's sinful attempt to play

God, to bridge the unbridgeable gap between here and there, to "communicate" without undergoing and reliving the stages of Christ's Passion. And Kierkegaard would have been seized with rage, had he been able to read in *Demian*: "Instead of crucifying oneself or somebody else, one can with solemn thoughts drink wine from a chalice and while doing it think the mystery of sacrifice." For Kierkegaard this substitution would have been stark paganism, as would be the Franciscan mysticism which we so frequently encounter in Hesse's works, the attempt to break the cage of individuation by expanding the soul so that it will become the lost All-ness again. It is quite characteristic that the Christian Hesse again and again substitutes for Christ's words "Love Thy neighbor as Thyself" the Buddhist's *"tat twam asi*, Love your neighbor for he is yourself."

His yearning for deliverance from the Ego, from the tyrannical dictate of temporality, has frequently led Hesse onto the road to India. The atmosphere of the Orient was familiar to him from his earliest childhood (both his father and his maternal grandfather were leading figures in the German-Swiss Indian Missionary Association; his mother, in fact, was born in Malabar), and this made access to the wisdom of the Orient particularly easy. But even without this stimulating heritage, Hesse would have found the way to Buddhism. For Buddhism offers the most radical possibility of undoing the curse of individuation, of annihilating the "idiotic one-after-the-other" by the postulation of the eternal simultaneity of Nirvana. What the East means to him, Hesse has expressed in his *Journey to the East*: "not only a country and something geographical, but the home and the youth of the soul, the everywhere and nowhere, the oneness of all times." However, it should be made quite plain that Buddhism (at least the Mahayana Buddhism with its extreme vision of the Universal Void) remains for Hesse a radical possibility, but by no means the solution to the problem. The extinction of the Ego, of the will to be, the kingdom of a lifeless and motionless eternity, in short: the realm of the Father, is only one station of the road to redemption, only one pole in the basic polarity of man's existence. Mozart's angry exhortation in *Steppenwolf*: "in the devil's name: live—that's just what you are to do" has rung down the curtain over the Nirvana, over Harry Haller's suicidal attempts to break out of the cage of individuation. But even in his Indian legend *Siddhartha* (Siddhartha, of course, is the historical name of the Gautama Buddha), which to many seemed a complete affirmation of the Buddhist faith, the dividing line is quite sharply drawn. It is again a quest for self-realization and salvation, and Siddhartha's travels lead through all the stages of self-fulfillment: life among the ascetic brethren who kill the desires of the flesh by flagellation in order to approach the "atman," life among the courtesans and nabobs of the big cities who, by draining the cup of pleasure to the last, hope to enter into the essence. But early in his travels Siddhartha has grasped the "ironical" solution: "Both, the mind and the senses, were pretty things behind which the last meaning was hidden, both had to be listened to, with both one had to play, neither of them was to be despised nor overrated." And when Siddhartha finally meets the great teacher Buddha, it dawns upon him that he cannot become his disciple either. For Buddha's division of the world into Samsara and Nirvana, deception and truth, phenomena and essence, time and eternity, is in Siddhartha's eyes no more than a pedagogical device. The true wisdom Siddhartha finds as a ferryman, as the link between the shores while watching the water and realizing "that the river is the same at all places, at its origin and its mouth, at the waterfalls, at the ferry point, at the rapids, in the ocean, in the mountains, everywhere, always simultaneous, and that for it there exists only presence, not the shadow of the past, nor the shadow of the future." This, then, is the solution: the stream itself is the coeval unity, the rhythm of fleeting moments is the everlasting presence.

This paradoxical oneness of the opposites, of time and eternity, individuation and Universal Self, life and death, mother and father, the apparent two which are essentially one, will show us again how wrong it is to interpret the polarity of Hesse's heroes in terms of narrow Freudianism. (It would be about as fitting to discover in the Indian gods Shiva and Vishnu "neurotic cases of split personalities.") That the tension between the poles is insoluble, that a definite fixation of the *condition humaine* is impossible, that the problem of man is beyond solution, can be learned from the very rhythm of Hesse's works. His books bear the relationship of complementary colors to each other. A great many of his readers found it baffling (and many even shocking) that *Siddhartha*, the serene Oriental legend in which all doubts seemed to be stilled, was followed by the weird Grand Guignol of the *Steppenwolf*. But the extreme amplitude of the pendulum's swing is just Hesse's unmistakable rhythm. "I have the misfortune that I always contradict myself"— *Demian*, the travel through "the hell in myself," is followed by *Siddhartha*. The companion piece to Siddhartha's saintly pursuit is the Witches' Sabbath of *Steppenwolf*. From Harry Haller's shrill dissonance, the pendulum swings to the tense but harmonious duo of Narcissus and Goldmund. But "since the paradox has to be risked again and again, the essentially impossible undertaken always anew," Goldmund's story, the love song to the fully experienced moment, to the intoxicated dance of life, required as a complementary color the lofty kingdom of Nirvana, the dead Void of eternity. It presented itself as the life story of Josephus Knecht in *The Glass Bead Game*.

This, Hesse's last work is—not only in volume—his most ambitious achievement. That it does not quite succeed has nothing to do with his artistic skill. The kingdom of eternity, "the extinction of the individual," cannot manifest itself in the framework of a realistic prose narrative however esoteric and legendary it may be. Without the help of a "magic theater," the attempt to render visible the place which is beyond space and time must end in failure, although, in Hesse's case, it is a most magnificent and noble failure. The story of Joseph Knecht takes place at a nowhere, in a completely secluded statehood of lay brethren whose only pursuit is learning and research. It takes place at no-time, at a period hundreds of years after the "age of wars" in which European civilization went to pieces. And the highest symbol of this citadel of the Spirit is the glass pearl game, "the sum total of everything spiritual and artistic, a sublime cult, an *Unio Mystica* of all the scattered branches of the *Universitas Litterarum*," a strange device by which, according to the highest rules of mathematics and musical harmony, one can "play" and vary all the distraught contents and values of mankind's spiritual manifestations into an all-embracing synchretism. If it can be fathomed at all (and it is Hesse's great achievement that it can—almost—be fathomed) it might be the invention of Chinese sages helped along by the great German mystic Jakob Boehme. In the glass pearl game the Spirit has—to use a Hegelian term—come to itself, it no longer creates but hovers in the immobility of self-meditation, introspection and auto-association. And its purest vessel is the Magister Ludi Josephus Knecht whose very name (Knecht—bondman) indicates that he is a function and not an individuality. (There has probably never before been written a "biography" which is so drained of *bios* and any individual psychology.) Here is the austere world of the father—until shortly before the end not a single woman appears on the pages of this book—and it is quite fitting for "life" in the Nirvana that Knecht refers to his own development as a succession of "awakenings" and "transcendencies." But this fortress of eternity, in which Knecht rises to the highest office, is only part of his "home." Against the advice of his superiors and colleagues he indulges in the study of history, the concern with the living moment, and at the height of his career he renounces his lofty office and leaves the world of the pure Spirit in order to dedicate himself to the modest service of an educator of a young man of the world. As Goldmund returns to the Father Narcissus after he has plumbed the depth of the mother world, so Knecht, who is Narcissus reborn, finally finds his way into life after he has plumbed the depth of the father world. The "ironic solution" is found again. And highly ironic is the end of the book. The very day Knecht enters into the service of life, he dies by drowning in a mountain lake. He, the unrivaled and idolized master of the great game, dies in the services of an immature youth who seems hardly worthy of this extreme sacrifice. But there is no futility in this irony. When the boy sees the master perish in the waters, the moment of his awakening has come: he knows that from now on he will have to live a life which will not only be his but that of the Magister Ludi as will. The transiency of man's existence, the fleeting instability of the moment, does not mark the victory of death but the triumph of eternal rebirth. Time, the one-after-the-other, is in the ironic vision eternity, the everlasting at-the-same-time. The "idiotic" rhythm of birth, unfolding and decay is the very heartbeat of the eternal, the great law of Hegel's dialectics: *Aufgehobensein* with the threefold meaning which the word *aufgehoben* carries in the German language: destroyed, preserved, and raised to a higher level.

In the summer of 1947 Hermann Hesse reached the biblical age. His latest work, magnificent in spite of its failures, seems to indicate that the storm has subsided. But we should not be unduly surprised if, provided that more than three score and ten are granted to him, he should continue to "contradict himself." He who has glanced so deeply into the chaos, who has felt so closely the grip of the "daimon," is not likely to catch more than a glimpse of the great calm in which the antinomies are resolved and reconciled. The balance is too precarious to be upheld, and even in the serene and austere pages of *The Glass Bead Game* we find confessions like the following: "There is no noble and lofty life without the knowledge of the devils and demons and without a perpetual battle against them." He is of the family of Dostoevsky, of those who tear out their hearts so that grace may be bestowed upon them. Peace in God, that is the goal, but the price they have to pay is tremendous. "Serenity"— this word sounds like an echo from the celestial city through Hesse's later books, and in his last work he has tried to catch its sublime reflection: "This serenity is neither frivolousness nor self-complacency, it is the highest wisdom and love, the affirmation of all reality, the wide-awakeness at the brink of all depths and abysses, the virtue of the saints and the knights." But only the one who is willing to realize and confess his sinfulness has a slight chance to become a saint. Exactly that Hesse has done all through his life: he has beaten his breast praying for grace. "There are two roads to salvation, the road of justice for the just ones, and the road of grace for the sinners. I who am a sinner have again committed the mistake of seeking the road of justice." (*Guest at the Spa*.) Only by an act of grace can serenity be envisaged; man cannot deserve it, he can only hope for it. The ironic attitude itself is not man's achievement, but the highest blessing that sainthood can bestow.

Again and again, Hermann Hesse has been compared and linked to Thomas Mann. To be sure, they are contemporaries. But the human attitude and the emotional climate of the two are vastly different. Hesse himself felt it very clearly when he drew in *The Glass Bead Game* the loving and astute portrait of Thomas von der Trave. (The Trave is the river on whose banks Lübeck, Thomas Mann's birthplace, is situated.) A sketchy comparison must of needs work injustice upon both of them. Thomas Mann—at least the mature Thomas Mann—is the apex of civilization; the demons, who are by no means alien to him, are subdued and neutralized. In this he is a true heir of Goethe. Hesse is the heir of Dostoevsky, whose concern is not man's autonomous dignity but man's saintliness, not justice but grace. The demons are on the loose in Dostoevsky as well as in Hesse. Thomas Mann, is, if these geospiritual generalizations be taken with a grain of salt, a Westerner, Hesse an Easterner. For Thomas Mann, the East is the danger zone which has to be warded off if man wants to live (Tadziu in *Death in Venice*, Mme. Chauchat and Naphta in the *Magic Mountain*), while Hesse has again and again seen the light arising from the East. Hesse has loudly proclaimed his love for Dostoevsky; Thomas Mann has recently published a beautiful essay on the great Russian under the characteristic title: "Dostoevsky— but in Moderate Doses." And the heroes of Thomas Mann's greatest *oeuvre* are Abram, Jacob and Joseph, proud men who have concluded a covenant with God, a Magna Charta of almost equal partners; the hero of Hesse's greatest *oeuvre* is Josephus Knecht, the humble servant. If the serenity for which Hesse so fervently strives is the "virtue of the saints and knights," Thomas Mann's serenity is knightly, Hermann Hesse's saintly.

There is nothing in Hesse's work to remind the reader of Thomas Mann's superior and, at times, olympic equanimity, the smoothness and ease of his transitions from one phase to the next, even in political matters. And if Thomas Mann's supreme vision is the Third Humanism, Hermann Hesse's is the eschatological Third Kingdom. Thomas Mann's work is undoubtedly wider in scope, richer with meaning and purer in outline; yet his heart never pulsates so visibly, audibly and close beneath the surface as does Hesse's. It is a tormented and struggling heart, beset by the tragic upheavals of the times, but much more thoroughly beset by the unalterable and timeless tragedy of man's existence. With the single exception of Franz Kafka, there is in contemporary German literature hardly anyone who has so valiantly and incessantly struggled with the angel as Hermann Hesse. Out of these struggles cries arose, but some of the purest and most beautiful poetry as well, some prose reminiscent of Mozart in its graceful serenity, short stories like "Knulp," "In the Old Sun," "How Beautiful Is Youth," where tensions and conflicts only grumble on in the bass accompaniment while the leading melody rises to lofty mirthfulness. These are the short moments of paradisial bliss which grace bestows upon the sinner. But the battlefield remains always close;

the demons are lurking, smashing the peace so hardly won. And it is as deeply moving as it is revealing to read in one of Hermann Hesse's recent poems:

> Heaps of shards and shambles far and wide:
> Thus ends the world, thus ends this life of mine.
> And I wished but to cry and to resign—
> If there were not this stubbornness inside,
>
> This stubbornness to ward off and to fight,
> Defiance deep deep in my heart below,
> And then my faith: that what torments me so
> Must, must one day turn into light.

Joseph Mileck

The Prose of Hermann Hesse: Life, Substance and Form

A bird's-eye view of Hermann Hesse's prose reveals three distinct periods, each of which represents a different stage in the course of the author's struggle with himself and with life and which reflects a correspondingly different phase in the mood of his creative activity and in the nature of his art. From this vantage point of distance and major trends rather than from the minutiae of individual works, one most readily perceives the continuity, the development and the gradual heightening of Hesse's prose in both its substance and its art.

The first of these three periods, the two decades preceding *Demian* (written in 1917), is one of uncertainty, irresolute groping and vague presentiment. These are the early years of a sensitive outsider who cannot yet, or will not, cope directly with his particular problem of existence.[1] He resorts instead to fantasy and withdraws into the realm of beauty, there to indulge in the extremes of late nineteenth-century aestheticism. The

[1] Hesse was born in Calw, Württemberg, 1877, the son of missionary parents and the grandson of the Pietist missionary and Indologist, Hermann Gundert. A hypersensitive, highly imaginative and very headstrong child, he was to prove a problem and a constant source of despair for both home and school. From 1891 to 1895 no educational institution would have him for long, nor could Hesse himself long tolerate any one institution. The period 1895–99 was spent in Tübingen and the subsequent five years in Basel; during these years, characterized primarily by lonely withdrawal and an inexorable passion to become a writer, Hesse devoted much of his time to bookselling, his chosen livelihood, more of it to avid reading, and most of his time and efforts to his own literary aspirations. It was while in Tübingen and during the first two years in Basel that *An Hour beyond Midnight* and *Hermann Lauscher* were written.

Reprinted from The German Quarterly, *vol. 27 (1954) by permission of the publisher and the author. Quotations have been rendered into English by the editor.*

prose of these years (*An Hour beyond Midnight,* 1899; *Hermann Lauscher,* 1901)[2] is enveloped in a weary, lethargic atmosphere pervaded by melancholy and intoxicating perfumes; the tone is eloquently oratorical, characterized by exclamatory remarks and rhetorical questions; the effusive language, replete with sensuous adjectives and adverbs, becomes languidly cadent; and the form is loose-knit, a random succession of vignettes and dramatic monologues held together primarily by a common, decadent romantic sprit: sentimental introversion and beauty-worship have become rather mawkish in their melodramatic exaggeration. This is the work of a talented beginner whose world of experience is still very limited and whose vibrant creative imagination is still immaturely entranced by the facile flow of beautiful language; in the absence of discipline and its restraint, the whole is sacrificed for the part, and potential art becomes picturesque patter. It was not long before Hesse himself termed this mode of writing the theatrics of nerve-artists and discounted it as

> sick, unintelligible and miserable . . . everything sounded like a ghostly idiotic whining, whose meaning was clear only to the initiated. One heard of temples, wildernesses, desert seas, and groves of cypress which were always being visited with heavy sighs by a timorous young man. One understood that it was all meant to be symbolic, but little was gained from that either.[3]

Beginning with Hesse's determination to escape the isolation of the introverted aesthete and with his consequent efforts in marriage to find a place for himself in the bourgeois world,[4] this initial, emotionally intense romanticism yields quite abruptly to a hardier, more appealing realism that recalls Gottfried Keller. *Peter Camenzind* (1904, *Gertrud* (1910) and to a lesser degree, *Rosshalde* (1914) continue the tradition of *Green Henry*, while the many *Gerbersau Novelles*[5] (and even the more tragic school novel, *Beneath the Wheel,* 1906), with their humorous and pleasantly ironic treatment of small-town life, are closely akin to the Seldwyla tales. The dream world of *An Hour beyond Midnight* with its affected

[2]Unless otherwise indicated the dates in parentheses are those of publication.

[3]"Karl Eugen Eiselein," *Nachbarn*, 1st ed., Berlin, 1908, p. 90.

[4]Hesse married Maria Bernoulli, daughter of an old and learned family of Basel, in the summer of 1904. That autumn, with literary success looming on the horizon, the young couple moved into a peasant's cottage in the village of Gaienhofen on the Bodensee. Although this rustic sojourn was to continue until 1912, bringing with it a new home and three sons, it was obvious to Hesse from almost the very beginning that his farmer ideal and his marriage, family and established home were not the real answers to his particular problems.

[5]*Gerbersau*, 2 vols., Tübingen and Stuttgart, 1949.

heroic pose, assumed martyrdom and pathos, its profuse colors, muted sounds and scented atmosphere, and the Hoffmannesque fusion of fantasy and reality, the cynicism and the morbid intimacy of *Hermann Lauscher*, are succeeded by a more invigorating rustic reality as mere shades become human beings and inertia and desperation yield to movement and humor. Hesse's prose now becomes more narrative, characterized by a hitherto completely lacking progressive continuity; his turbid stream of mournful adjectives is contained, and his language becomes more forceful, clearer and crisper.

It is in this vein that Hesse continues until his crisis of 1916–17.[6] The decade to follow, the second of the three periods, marks the most dramatic and most critical years of his life. Distraught by the sudden accumulation of tensions, by the war, by the growing discord in his marriage and by his father's death, and disturbed by his own complacency and by his indifference to matters of the world at large, Hesse is now compelled to realize that, in his desire to make existence less painful, he had theretofore deliberatley avoided probing too deeply into the true nature of his inner discord and had blinded himself to the morally and spiritually poverty-stricken world about him. Incapable of further escapist pretense, he now repudiates as sham the civilization around him. Like Veraguth (*Rosshalde*), Hesse leaves the comfortable fold of the bourgeois world for the more difficult hermitic existence of an outsider reconciled to his lot[7]; and in a desperate and determined attempt to find himself and inner peace, he finally begins systematically to diagnose his inner conflict, to go his long-shunned "Way Within."

Escape becomes quest, and in quest Hesse's inner problems resolve themselves into the basic *malaise humaine*, into the tension between *Geist* (spirit) and *Natur* (nature). For years he was to vacillate between these poles, periodically acclaiming one, then the other, and then giving preference to neither, and all the while never ceasing to envisage a

[6]Finding it unendurable to continue his established mode of existence in Gaienhofen, and recognizing the impossiblity of his efforts to be both a man of fantasy and a *Bürger*, Hesse fled to India in the summer of 1911, vainly seeking the perspective and respite of distance. Shortly after his return to Europe at the close of 1911, the family took up residence in the outskirts of Bern. During the war matters went from bad to worse: an outspoken pacifist, Hesse soon fell into serious disrepute; his youngest son was severely ill for more than a year; his wife became mentally ill; and to retain his own mental health, Hesse himself underwent psychoanalytic treatment (November 1916 to May 1917). Hesse finally left Bern in the spring of 1919, again to become a lonely, homeless figure; his wife had been put into an asylum and his children into the homes of friends.

[7]Quitting Bern, a burned out literatus, Hesse found a quiet retreat in Montagnola, Tessin (May, 1919). In rented rooms in the Casa Camuzzi he began painfully to take stock of himself and life and assiduously to devote himself to his art. In the course of the next decade it was only intermittently, and then for but brief periods, that Hesse emerged from this refuge.

harmonious accord of both, though well aware that such was hardly meant for him. In *Demian* (1919) it is *Geist* with its self-realization and a Nietzschean emphasis upon the willfulness of the superior being which is acclaimed. Very nearly as brief as it was intense, this ideal was to culminate in the *Amor fati,* the will to suffer and be lonely of *Zarathustra's Return* (1919), only to be brushed aside almost immediately thereafter. *Geist* as a guiding principle of life could only mean greater individuation and more painful isolation; as yet, Hesse lacked the firm conviction and the inner fortitude necessary to continue to embrace this principle and to endure its consequences. The immediate reaction was as extreme as the initial impulse; the assertive Nietzschean activism yields suddenly to a Schopenhauer-like passivity, restless quest to a quietistic acceptance, self-realization to a yearning for self-obliteration. Nature with its "experience" is as demanding as it is impossible for Klein (*Klein and Wagner,* 1920), and respite is found only in the nirvana of a will-less surrender.

But Hesse was as ill-prepared to accept Klein's resolution as he had been to follow the path of Demian. Envisaging more possibilities and giving precedence to neither *Geist* nor *Natur*, he proceeds with Klingsor (*Klingsor's Last Summer*, 1920) to revel in the intoxication of both. Acknowledging the reality, the goodness and the necessity of both realms of experience, *Siddhartha* (1922) advances yet another stage: while Klingsor fails to emerge from his revelry, Siddhartha, exhausting and transcending both "the accidental ego of thought" and "the accidental ego of the senses," achieves a condition of the soul which knows only unity, affirmation and humble service. *Guest at the Spa* (1924), however, is a reminder that resolutions are more easily visualized than experienced. Hesse soberly accepts as a fact that, despite all efforts to the contrary, his existence would probably continue to be a restless tension, a constant vacillation between life's opposing poles. It is the most acute stage of this continued tension that *Steppenwolf* (1927) records. In his own words, Hesse had reached another of those "stages of life where the spirit tires of itself, abdicates its throne and lets nature, chaos and all that is animalistic reign free."[8] With recuperation from this embittered and desperate state of mental exhaustion, this trying period of quest and indecision ends. A tired and wiser man, fully aware of the value, the necessity of humor, Hesse was now prepared at last resolutely to acclaim *Geist* and to make of it—that part of human nature so repeatedly deemed the very bane of existence during the difficult years immediately following *Demian*—his guiding principle.

The new, more vigorous approach to life and its problems of this

[8]"Nachwort an meine Freunde," *Krisis, Ein Stück Tagebuch,* Berlin, 1928, p. 81.

second period brings with it a new, more vigorous stage in Hesse's creative activity. The years from *Demian* to *Steppenwolf* are impulsively prolific; with reckless abandon the author gives free rein to his creative urge, yielding fully to the mood and necessity of the moment. The resultant abrupt change in both the substance and art of his prose extends Hesse's literary horizons far beyond the previous conventional range, and the course of this new, more dramatic phase of his writing becomes very unpredictable, characterized by spasmodic transition rather than by gradual progression.

With *Demian*, the once rather innocent writer of light fiction suddenly becomes a disconcerting, problematic seeker whose unusually complex expressionistic art all but defies satisfactory interpretation. The simplicity of language and clarity of thought which had become characteristic of Hesse's writings are now obscured in a nebulous atmosphere of abstruse Freudian symbolism. Hesse becomes so engrossed in his psychological self that his art tends to suggest the efforts of an analytic talent more than the work of a creative artist. *Demian*[9] and the novella *Klein and Wagner* would almost prompt one to think of clinical reports in artistic guise, rather than of works of art with psychological implications. On the other hand, though obviously still under the influence of *Demian* and its symbolism, *Klingsor's Last Summer*, a chaotic rhapsody suggests a return to the decadent romanticism of *An Hour Beyond Midnight*; again the atmosphere is scented, the scene removed and feverish; and though much more vibrant and cohesive, the whole once more becomes a heterogeneous maze of melodramatic vignettes.

The unpredictable course of Hesse's art during this period is even more evident in the sudden transition from *Klingsor's Last Summer* to *Siddhartha*, from intoxication and random spontaneity to contemplation and severe artistry, from a romantic fragment to a work of art, classical in the symmetry of its form, in the stylized pattern of its expression and in the lofty simplicity of its language. The equally abrupt transition and descent from the elevated plane of *Siddhartha* to the diary-like intimacy, the capricious, comic realism and the acrid *leitmotif* technique of *Guest at the Spa* is romantically ironical in its bizarre effect. Even more startling are the extremes of the *Steppenwolf*; here Hesse's "faith to oneself" climaxes in a fascinating confusion of symbol and irony, fantasy and realism.

As the agitation of *Steppenwolf* subsides, the third and final period of Hesse's life and art begins. The storm is past, inner strife has been diagnosed and decisions have been made; Hesse is prepared to leave his

---

[9]Though not published until 1919, this novel was written (as indicated earlier) in 1917, while Hesse was still in the care of Dr. J. B. Lang, a student of Jung; from November 1916 to May 1917 seventy-two consultations took place.

hermitage and in remarriage to adjust himself anew to life.[10] After years of painful growth he had finally reached that last vital turning point in life beyond which *Werden* (becoming) becomes *Entwerden* (becoming not), the self is slowly transcended and the unity of reality ultimately experienced. The years since have been contented years of quiet retirement, contemplation and close communion with nature. It is only now that Hesse at last finds the peace of sincere acceptance of self and life.

A corresponding change can be detected in Hesse's art of these latter years. While the *Geist* and *Natur* dichotomy continues to be the vital issue in his world of thought, it is no longer the acutely personal problem it once was. It is in the milder, the more detached manner of recollection, rather than in further quest, that the question is reconsidered in *Narcissus and Goldmund* (1930). Just as frequently in the past, both poles of life are again acknowledged and affirmed by Hesse, but his previous attitude toward the dichotomy of reality, his resignation to a life of vacillation, is supplanted by a new, more determined adjustment to life: despite distractions the individual must obey the prevailing impulse of his being, must take and cling to that path which the predominant aspect of his nature would impel him to choose. Both the *Naturkind* (child of nature) and the *Geistesmensch* (man of the spirit) must and will basically remain such as they are; each must be prepared unflinchingly to suffer the lot of his kind, and for either to be irresolute and to attempt, in curiosity or desperation, to do otherwise would be to foster a perpetual *Steppenwolf*-like inner dissension. Determined as he was to suffer this inner discord no longer, Hesse's future road was obvious to him; it could only be that of all *Travelers to the East* (1932), the way of *Geist*.

The Glass Bead Game (1943) represents the final stage on this road. *Geist*, formerly stressed primarily in terms of the individual and of self-expression, is now finally viewed in terms of humanity and of self-justification. Cultivated for its own sake in Castalia-like isolation from tangible reality and life at large, *Geist* can only deteriorate into a purposeless activity, doomed to perish in its own sterility. Only when it becomes a vital formative factor in human existence, when it is mellowed

[10]Hesse married again in 1931. Thanks to the generosity of close friends, he was now able to leave his Casa Camuzzi retreat, once more to live in a home and garden he could call his own. With the rise of Hitler's régime, Hesse's popularity in Germany gradually waned. For a number of years the Nazis condescended to tolerate him, largely because he refrained from any public pronouncement of his antipathy toward the Third Reich (in contrast to his severe criticism of Germany during the First World War; see *Krieg und Frieden,* Zürich, 1946), but by 1937 publication of Hesse's books had almost ceased, and in 1943 they were finally added to the official blacklist. Since 1945, however, Hesse has again become one of the most widely read and respected authors in Germany. Notwithstanding, and despite frail health and failing eyesight, he has continued his humble existence in Montagnola, still devoted to his art and patiently tending his garden.

by a humanitarian spirit of love, service and sacrifice like that exemplified in Knecht's way of life can *Geist* serve its ultimate, its true purpose and thereby justify itself and those who promote it.

In keeping with this new adjustment to life and this more dispassionate attitude toward what he regards as its basic problem, Hesse's once explosive inspiration and once impulsively prolific creative activity are expressed to a greater degree as conscious craftsmanship and less as ready productivity. Reflecting his slower tempo of life and more orderly existence, his art is now less dramatic in its tensions and much more narrative in its new, expansive nature; its atmosphere is less charged, becoming progressively more rare; language is less constrained, vocabulary is marked more than ever by poetic simplicity, syntax becomes more playfully involved and symbolism even more prevalent and profoundly enigmatic. In all three of the remaining tales it is a romantic spirit which again prevails: a romantic spirit purged of its former decadence, become mature and mellow, wider in its scope, deeper in its thought, less aware of itself, and more conscious of its art. While very modern in its psychological depth, it is to German Romanticism's best tradition of story-telling, to that of *Franz Sternbald's Travels* and *Presentiment and the Present*, that *Narcissus and Goldmund* belongs. *Journey to the East*, reverting briefly to the episodic-tale-form most peculiar to the second period, is a playful fantasia which could have been written by Novalis and would have been acclaimed by Tieck. And *The Glass Bead Game* immediately recalls Goethe's *Wilhelm Meister*, both in substance and in its structure and baroque proportions; it is romantic in its loose composition, in its fragmentary nature, in the innocence and naiveté of its idyllic setting, in the *clair-obscur* of its symbolism, its efforts to give expression to the otherwise inexpressible, and romantic in its dream, its glass-bead game with its idea of universality.

While Hesse's prose passes through the three phases just outlined, the center about which his creative activity revolves and about which his vivid imagination and his unusual mastery of language weave their varied tapestry remains constant. This nucleus is the *individual* as opposed to society, its masses and its institutions; it is, more immediately, Hermann Hesse *himself*. Those early, simpler years of childhood that precede rude awakening to reality and its distressing incongruities are nostalgically recalled; youth with its excruciating years of awakening is reexperienced in all its original intensity; the plight of modern man, of the intellectual and of the artist in particular, within the framework of a culture in decline, the predicament of human nature become problematic amid the stress of an age abnormally out of joint, are graphically and painfully portrayed. For this nucleus a wide range of time and space provides an ever changing setting: the Occident yields to the Orient, commonplace reality to the magic realm of nowhere, and the Middle Ages and the distant future are as immediate and vital as is the present. This fluid, diversified and yet continuous whole represents the Odyssey of Hesse's changing self, and it is in this, its intimately egocentric nature, that his art bears the stamp of its age: an age of cultural decline, of spiritual and moral distress, and of extreme loneliness.

Like many of his fellow individualists, idealists and humanitarians, Hesse was unwilling and unable to live in accord with the soulless mass civilization emerging from this alleged decline. Between an age and these, its most sensitive spirits, there developed an antipathy which was to change the course of art: the inner and outer tensions and the loneliness which are normally part of the artist's lot became acute; normal introversion became impassioned introspection, and art began to lose that balance between the ego and the world which is peculiar to it at its best. Hesse himself was caught up in this trend to such an extent that *Bekennen* (confession) and *Aufrichtigkeit* (honesty), and not beauty, became the motivating factors in his creative activity; his art became confessional in form and therapeutic in function—his contribution to what he himself has termed the transitional literature of a transitional period.[11]

While time alone will ultimately confirm or disprove Hesse's severe (ironic?) criticism of his own art, the inordinately egocentric nature of this art is an immediate and inescapable fact. Like a hall of mirrors the author's works never cease to reflect his own image.[12] His pre-*Demian* heroes are made of soft stuff; they are predominantly aesthetes who live only in dreams, hopes and anticipation and who shrink from realization; they are self-preoccupied, temperamental artists who are paralyzed by chronic indecision and who indulge in romantic morbidity. They are outsiders consumed by their own loneliness, misfits to whom the *ars vivendi* and the *ars amandi* are foreign, timid souls who ask too little of life, yet expect too much of it, and hence live in perpetual frustration and disillusionment. Heroes of this type are the sentimental cynic Lauscher, the would-be *Naturkind* Camenzind, the timorous composer Kuhn (*Gertrud*), and even the more resolute painter Veraguth (*Rosshalde*) and the more stoical wanderer Knulp—and such a man was Hesse too.

While Hesse's figure still looms behind the person and fate of each of his pre-*Demian heroes*, in the decade to follow, author and hero gradually merge in a poetic, autobiographical fusion. Wayward Klein, frenzied Klingsor and, in particular, the rheumatic *Guest at the Spa* and the desperate *Steppenwolf* are hardly more than flesh of Hesse's person

---

[11] *Kurgast; Die Nürnberger Reise,* Zürich, 1946, p. 224.

[12] The major portion of Hesse's works is written in the *Ich* form.

and spirit of his being. Like Hesse, now in serious quest of self-knowledge and of self-expression, these new heroes shed their lethargy and take fate by the forelock. The outside world has more than ever become a mere setting for the prolonged drama of Hesse's *Ich*.

It is only in *Siddhartha* and in his last novels, *Narcissus and Goldmund* and *The Glass Bead Game*, that Hesse seems to have managed to extricate himself sufficiently from this engrossment with his own immediate, personal problems to enable him to mould his art with the care necessary to insure it, beyond any doubt, against the wear of time and to give to its substance some of those more universal implications inherent in all truly great art.

Recalling my introductory remark that Hesse's prose falls into three distinct periods, each of which represents a different stage in his struggle with himself and with life at large and each of which reflects a correspondingly different phase in the mood of his creative activity and in the nature of his art, the material just presented might be summarized as follows: Until *Demian*, evasive groping characterizes Hesse's adjustment to life, and vague presentiment characterizes his insight into his inner discord. His creative mood is languid and sentimental, his art is traditional, even imitative, with a distinctive lyrical quality. The period from *Demian* to *Steppenwolf* is one of self-imposed isolation, of determined quest and of decision; self-analysis is exhausted and the *Geist* and *Natur* problem is plumbed. The creative mood of this pregnant period is tense and serious, and inspiration is impulsive; Hesse's art now becomes more original, more modern, and decidedly dramatic. The remaining years are quiet ones of final adjustment; having learned to accept and to affirm both himself and life, Hesse becomes progressively less concerned with himself and more concerned with humanity and the individual's obligations to humanity. With this gradual subsiding of life's tensions, his creative mood becomes more sober and tranquil, stormy inspiration yields to conscious craftsmanship, and in its new expansiveness and measured tread Hesse's art acquires a truly epic quality.

Ralph Freedman

Romantic Imagination: Hermann Hesse as a Modern Novelist

I

Hermann Hesse's debt to the romantic tradition is a critical commonplace. It is perhaps less often recognized that he is also a distinctly modern novelist. Hesse's modernity is not confined to his period of preoccupation with Jungian psychoanalysis or to his brush with expressionism in *Steppenwolf* and elsewhere. Nor is it exclusively a negative principle: a rejection of contemporary reality and a search for new values, as in the monastery of Narcissus or in the futuristic-medieval Castalia of *The Glass Bead Game*. Rather, in aesthetic and moral terms, Hesse's modernity is found in his manner of formulation romantic thought and techniques. His aesthetic sensibility recalls Novalis and Jean Paul, but his way of implementing this sensibility is representative of a contemporary attitude.

A personal comment in a preface to his selected works (publication of which was abandoned upon the author's insistence) trenchantly states Hesse's own sense of his place in the tradition of German letters: ''The story as disguised poetry, the novel as a borrowed label for the attempts of poetic natures to express their feelings of self and of the world—that was specifically German and Romantic, and here I knew myself to be guilty as well.'' This guilt, Hesse continues, is shared by many of his contemporaries and predecessors, for German prose is an enticing instrument for making music, to whose lure many poets have succumbed

Reprinted by permission of the Modern Language Association of America from PMLA, *vol. 73 (1958). Quotations have been rendered into English by the editor.*

without realizing that lyricism must be accompanied by a gift for story-telling.[1]

Although Hesse's awareness of his "lyrical" approach to fiction was often accompanied by anguish, he also felt that in a time of mechanization there is a great need for a survival of romantic values, of which he saw himself as the last standard-bearer.[2] He admired Thomas Mann's ability, in *Doktor Faustus*, to equip his showcases lavishly with characters and scenes to create a world or profusion against which Leverkühn's organized and transparent inner world stood out in sharp relief.[3] But Hesse's work as a whole seems to invoke Novalis and Hölderlin—or Indian and Chinese thinkers who, it seemed to him, expressed similar ideas—to show that the lively world of experience finds its most subtle reflection in a heightened vision of the self caught by the magic of art. In a preface to an American edition of *Demian*, Mann himself distinguished between his own intellectual and Hesse's lyrical bent: "Very likely in my own country I was nothing but a gray sparrow of the intellect among a flock of emotional Harz songsters . . . . But Hesse? What ignorance, what lack of culture, to banish this nightingale from its German grove, this lyric poet whom Mörike would have embraced with emotion, who has produced from our language images of purest and most delicate form."[4]

Hesse's drive to penetrate to the depth of the human psyche stamps him as both a moralist obsessed with the contradictions inherent in his time and an artist determined to present these contradictions as they are immediately reflected in the human self. Thus it is precisely the paradoxical relationship of the Swabian lyricist to the "spheres of the Viennese erotological 'analytical psychology' " enjoyed by Mann in *Narcissus and Goldmund* that accurately defines Hesse's place.[5] In his amazingly faithful translation of the Romantic tradition Hesse may be outside the

---

[1] *Betrachtungen* (Berlin: S. Fischer, 1928), pp. 172–173. Hesse's lyricism is stressed by Ernst R. Curtius, who points out that Hesse desired neither aesthetic nor social ties but rather sought immediate self-expression. Hence, Curtius concludes, Hesse's works are lyrical rather than epic, for the world implied by the latter is absent in them ("Hermann Hesse," *Kritische Essays zur europäischen Literatur* [Bern: A. Francke, 1950], pp. 212–213).

[2] In *Die Nürnberger Reise* (*Journey to Nuremberg*) (1928), Hesse identifies the romantic spirit with an antimodern spirit and readily allies himself with it (*Gesammelte Dichtungen* [Berlin-Zürich: Suhrkamp Verlag, Fretz and Wasmuth Verlag, 1952], IV, 128–129—hereafter cited as *Dichtungen*).

[3] Letter to Thomas Mann, 12 Dec. 1947 in *Briefe* (Berlin: Suhrkamp, 1951), pp. 269–270.

[4] See Foreword, *Demian* (New York: Henry Holt, 1948 [written April 1947)], pp. vi–viii.

[5] *Demian* (New York), p. x.

main stream of the European novel that extends from Flaubert to Joyce, Gide, and Mann (Curtius, pp. 215 ff.). In his pointed analysis of the self in a divided age, however, Hesse is part of that generation in German letters which made its debut in the last decade of the nineteenth century.

A romantic sensibility pervades most of Hesse's work, although different facets of romanticism are found meaningful in different periods. His reading list contained in *A Library of World Literature* (1929), as well as his anthologies and essays, reveals great love for writers associated with the romantic tradition, including, in addition to Goethe, Jean Paul Richter, Novalis, Hölderlin, Bettina von Arnim, Clemens Brentano, Eichendorff, E. T. A. Hoffman, and Mörike.[6] In Hesse's early work, romantic motifs are associated with the rarefied symbolism of *fin de siècle* theory and practice, whether in the first collection of lyrical prose poems and fairy tales, *An Hour beyond Midnight* (1899) or in the slightly more unified *Hermann Lauscher* (1901).[7] Although the intention of this latter work had been to question aestheticism by reconquering "a piece of the world," Hesse allows his hero to be sacrificed at the altar of beauty in that losing battle against a hostile world made familiar by his later writings.[8] In the successful early novels of his "adjusted" Gaienhofen period, like *Beneath the Wheel* (1905–06) and *Rosshalde* (1912–14), Hesse's approach seems to have been often akin to the rural realism of Gottfried Keller.[9] But even in this period the themes he deals with are largely those elaborated later in mysticism, psychoanalysis, and metaphysics: the conflict of opposites, of self and world, God and Satan, which must be reconciled lest they lead to the individual's disintegration.[10]

The resolution of conflict, ultimately in mystical vision or aesthetic imagination, is Hesse's most consistent romantic theme, which extends

[6]*A Library of World Literature* (Zürich: Werner Classen, 1945), pp. 40–48.

[7]Hesse readily admits the influence of Maeterlinck on his first prose work, but claims that he had not read George's *Hirtengedichte* until a few months later. In fact, he suggests in retrospect that his reluctance about aestheticism in *Hermann Lauscher* can be attributed not only to doubts about Maeterlinck's self-enclosed form but also to his rejection of the preciosity and egocentricity which, to his mind, were involved in the cult surrounding Stefan George ("Geleitwort," *Eine Stunde hinter Mitternacht* (*An Hour beyond Midnight*), 2nd ed. [Zürich: Fretz und Wasmuth, 1941], pp. 9–11).

[8]Ibid., p. 11. For criticisms of the aesthetic point of view, see the discussions between Lauscher and Drehdichum in "Lulu," *Hermann Lauscher* (München: Albert Langen, 1920), pp. 102–112. For Lauscher's martyrdom in the service of beauty see also pp. 189–190.

[9]Hesse remarked that Gottfried Keller's technique demonstrates conspicuously many romantic traits (*Hermann Lauscher*, p. 195).

[10]For a brief summary of Hesse's work in his first two periods, including his themes and models, see Joseph Mileck, "The Prose of Hermann Hesse: Life, Substance, and Form," *GQ*, XXVII (May 1954), 165–166. [Pp. 31–32 of this volume—*Ed.*]

into the culminating novels of his old age. Although the landmarks of his life, like his journey to India in 1911, his sessions with the Jungian analyst Dr. Lang in 1917–19, or his rejection of psychoanalysis after 1927, mark changes in Hesse's sensibility and thought, his work continues to focus on a constant reappraisal of the clash of self and world and of conflicting forces within the self.[11] This reappraisal manifests itself mystically and psychoanalytically in *Demian* (1919). It appears as a nightmare of schizophrenic dissolution in *Steppenwolf* (1927) and, in less harsh terms, in the pilgrimage of *Journey to the East* (1932). In *Narcissus and Goldmund* (1930), self and world, soul and intellect, are juxtaposed in an allegory deliberately based on a romantic setting and form. Even in *The Glass Bead Game* (1943), a Magic Mountain and an intellectually rarefied atmosphere do not obscure the basic striving for a transcendence of man and world in a higher vision that might provide resolution or despair.

II

Two titles, *The Way Within* and *In Sight of Chaos*, suggest the direction of Hesse's approach. For especially in his postwar novels, Hesse has been concerned with the inner world turned inside out, yielding not only sequences of dreams, memories, or hallucinations per se but also the world of underlying perception, dissolving and recomposing itself in the self's inner landscape. If Hölderlin's Hyperion and Novalis' Heinrich reflected directly their encounters and experiences in exclamations of feeling and symbolic images, Hesse's protagonists show their experience of the industrial civilization he despised in an internal perspective.[12]

As it confronts the world, the self seeks to absorb its opponent. In a frightening scene in "A Dream Sequence," included in *Fairy Tale* (1919), the protagonist seizes society's most offensive exemplar and hammers him to his liking (III, 329–330). Characters opposing an alien social reality, whether in *Beneath the Wheel*, "Klein and Wagner," or *Steppenwolf*, are dissolved either through death or schizophrenia. This alien reality or "world" is variously identified with anything seemingly external to the self, including objects of perception, nonintuitive reasoning, social pressures, mercantilism, and so on; in short, it is a very wide concept which includes the very world of perception as well as

---

[11]For a full discussion of Hesse's use of polarities cf. Peter Heller, "The Creative Unconscious and the Spirit: A Study of Polarities in Hesse's Image of the Writer," *MLF*, XXXVIII (March–June 1953), 28–40.

[12]See e.g., *Die Nürnberger Reise, Dichtungen*, IV, 165–166. Hereafter, unless otherwise identified, parenthetical volume and page numbers in the text will refer to *Dichtungen*.

contemporary reality.[13] If, then, the self attempts to come to terms with the world by uniting it with its psyche, it can be successful only if the experiences absorbed by the self are not inimical to ''nature,'' that is, to sensual reality. In *Narcissus and Goldmund*, the natural world of *Bilder* within the self (of Goldmund) is easily linked with experiences of nature; only then can the intellect (Narcissus) intervene and impose form upon the sensual-natural material. But if the ''world'' is immediately identified with a nonintuitive, antisensual, or even dehumanized world, the kind of failure must result which Hesse describes in his *Journey to Nuremberg* (1928) (IV, 149 and passim). As in perception both form and sensuous content are joined in the self, so the tension between a sensual self and a hostile, desensualized world must also be joined in the self. Hesse is thus forced to deal with the conflict of self and world, sense and intellect, quite as much in psychological as in social or intellectual terms.[14]

Translated into an inner conflict, Hesse's opposition of self and world is portrayed not so much in dramatic action as in symbolic and allegorical self-representation. For Novalis, the artist represents himself in an object; he depicts his inner condition and by this act transmutes the object through which he is externalized into a manifestation of the infinite self, the visible work of art. For Hesse, numerous instances of self-representation, exhibited in drawings, statues, or fictional biographies, often mirror the author's or hero's self (or the themes of his life) directly and issue in schizophrenic distortions and symbolic manipulations more intense than those envisaged by Novalis.

In his scattered remarks on the purpose of poetry, and hence of the novel as a high form of organic or poetic expression, Novalis considered the dissolution of alien existence in that of the poet's self an important function of poetry. Awakening another individuality (or more often individualities) within the self, the poet becomes a supreme mimic. In this way, alien conflicts are incorporated within the self, contradictory forces or points of view are juxtaposed in the figure of the poet.[15] Hesse also identifies images and characters with external figures or points of view, but for him this process is associated with a psychological or symbolic enactment of inner conflict. In *Steppenwolf*, for example, points of view intersect, each showing a different aspect of Haller's self:

[13]See Hesse's remark in *Die Nürnberger Reise* that poetry (an intuitive, sensual apprehension of the world) must lead to ''conflict and dissociation from reality'' (*Dichtungen*, IV, 149).

[14]This explains the dual conflict which is so often seen in Hesse, that is, the conflict of the self with the external world and the conflict within the self. As the self seeks to absorb the world the two oppositions coincide. Cf. Heller, pp. 28 f.

[15]According to Novalis, the novel is natural, that is, organic poetry. Allegory, in which the relationship of ideas to represented images is logical rather than organic, belongs to artificial poetry.

the editor's introduction, Haller's notebooks and poems, the *Steppenwolf* treatise. In each case, we gain an insight into the mechanism of the *Outsider*; his soul is a composite picture of all these perspectives. Characters are likewise identified with various aspects of Haller's self, such as Hermine, Maria, Pablo, and others. They are guides and teachers, in the sense of Klingsor and Alabanda, but they are really images of conflicting attitudes imposed upon Haller's inhibited personality. Towards the end, these figures are more abstractly conceived when, in the Magic Theater, Pablo turns into Mozart and Hermine into a mirrored image. Indeed, the concluding sequence shows Hesse's method of presenting the subconscious symbolically through shifting images. The peep show scenes in Pablo's theater, clearly reflections of Haller's subconscious mind, are literally ejected from mirrors.

Some of the methods governing *The Glass Bead Game* are parallel to those in *Steppenwolf*, except that different values are attached to them. An objective chronicler focuses on the external characteristics of Knecht and the world of *Castalia*. His point of view is matched by Knecht's internal biography drawn in the fictional "Biographies," by the poems appended to the novel, and by the "symbolic end." This composite of different perspectives is augmented by a further parallel of mirroring. Knecht is reflected in a variety of figures—Plinio Designiori, the Old Music Master, Master Thomas von der Trave, Pater Jakobus, the Elder Brother, or even his friend Tegularius—who in one way or another tend to represent the various problems and conflicts, as well as emotions, with which Knecht is confronted at different moments of his career. But the tensions dominating Knecht's inner world, as well as the themes of the novel, are most succinctly expressed in the Game of Glass Beads itself, which in its intellectual refinement represents the idea of unity in multiplicity associated with Novalis. The objective perspective is mirrored in an internal perspective; therefore, the function of the Game of Glass Beads is comparable to that of the *Steppenwolf* treatise, despite the great differences between the two novels in terminology and outlook.

An analytic sharpening of self-representation manifests itself particularly in Hesse's use of the "other self," which regulates the self both morally and aesthetically. Besides functioning as a Freudian superego of Jungian collective unconscious, this higher aspect of the self acts as a daimon who guards the activities of the self and comments upon them ironically. Mirroring thus occurs not only through the reflection of the self in other figures—guides or teachers like Demian, Louis in *Klingsor's Last Summer,* or Leo in *The Journey to the East*—but also through representations of the inner man in which hidden faculties of control are revealed.

Hesse's diverse identifications of the relationship of the artist's self to his experiences primarily turn on the opposition of sense and intellect which is associated with that of dark and light, mother and father, sensuality and ascetic control. An analysis of Hesse's use of these categories shows these oppositions to be elusive. As has been frequently noted, *Geist*, both spirit and intellect, includes many diverse connotations ranging from the regulating, paternal force of "control" to the destructive power of a rationalistic mass culture, although it often also includes the clarity of a divinely rational spirit; its counterpoint, *Seele*, on the other hand, is both sensuality and soul, associated with sexuality, debauch, sense experience, and the recognition of the mother image or the collective unconscious. There is no doubt about Hesse's primary impulses: in *Narcissus and Goldmund* integration was to have taken place chiefly through *Seele* (soul), in *The Glass Bead Game* through *Geist* (mind). But intuitively Hesse weighs his evidence on the side of *Seele*. Sexuality, the world of the senses, must be experienced in its wholeness; it must be reflected in the magic vision of the imagination that leads to art—the lesson of *Steppenwolf*. Sensuality makes possible artistic integration, but it must be wedded to the ordering intellect or else chaos will result—the lesson of *Narcissus and Goldmund*. But in *The Glass Bead Game* Knecht turns his back on the paradise of *Geist* and reenters sensual nature, there to find his death. *Castalia* is a wholly masculine world; it is also an arid one. Indeed, although Hesse greatly admired *Geist* and thought it indispensable to artistic creation, he nowhere allows it to triumph in the end: neither in the intuitive vision of harmony in *Siddhartha* (1923) nor in the ethereal clarity of *The Glass Bead Game*.

The interaction of *Geist* and *Seele* is woven into the fabric of Hesse's major novels. Continuously requiring and counteracting one another, these opposing poles act as antinomies that recall Fichte's *Wechselwirkung*, the thought underlying Novalis' and Hölderlin's *Fragments*, and even Schiller's opposition of form and content to be reconciled in the play of art. In consonance with this analogy, Hesse views the artist's content, the material of *Seele*, as the sensual component, which he extends to entail sexuality. In "A Dream Sequence," the symbol for art is a woman, mysterious but decidedly sexual, who dissolves into a child as the artist carries her into another realm (III, 330–331). In *Fairy Tale,* the artist's song is made possible by a kiss which from then on inspires his art (III, 296). Indeed, the artist's search is intrinsically sexual, and sequences of debauch, in "Augustus" or *Klingsor's Last Summer,* in *Knulp* (1915) or *Klein and Wagner*, in *Siddharta, Demian, Steppenwolf,* or *Narcissus and Goldmund,* act as moments of essential experience, as the matter that goes into the making of art. The use of sense encounters absorbed by the hero of romantic fiction, in *Heinrich von Ofterdingen* or Eichendorff's *Taugenichts*, is heightened and intensified by Hesse, because sense experience is rendered also in sexual terms.

Hesse's concept of *Seele* in the double sense of nonintellectual, intuitive vision (*Schau*) and sensuality enables him to move from the opposition of creative sensuality (feminine) and controlling intellectuality (masculine) to their integration, literally, in an Oversoul, a transcendental soul. On the way to this union of *Seele* and *Geist* in a heightened self, Hesse's characters often reenact Christian salvation from and through the immersion in sensuality. This search for fulfillment, which for Hesse seems to involve both the Augustinian notion and Nietzschean transcendence, is shown in many different ways: in Klein's and Knecht's deaths by water, in Goldmund's creation of works of art by combining *Seele* with Narcissus' control of *Geist*, in Sinclair's final vision and Demian's resolving kiss, in Siddhartha's maturity. In these examples, *Seele* is raised from a psychological to a metaphysical level of existence as resolution approaches; it is transferred from a sensual to a transcendental plane. But this transcendental *Seele* is not unrelated to the *Seelenwelt* of the artist's material. In her double function of mistress and mother, woman embodies for Hesse the libidal force which represents the artist's material (the world of nature which he must incorporate and merge with his own) and the maternal goal, the *Urgrund,* in which salvation and aesthetic reconciliation are found. "We all," Hesse says in his introduction to *Demian,* "come from the same abyss" (III, 102). In the womb, the original matrix of experience, whatever its possibilities of chaos may be, integration is reached. By acquiring a vision of this ground, the poet can attain to *Seele* in its transcendental function. He can, with Novalis, become the "transcendental physician."

As the individual self is mirrored in a universal self, so the libidal sense-self is mirrored in its transcendental representation. In Hesse's identifications, this higher self becomes simultaneously the unity of Yoga mysticism, Jung's collective unconscious, and the unity of opposites of romantic thought. In this way, the transcendental *Seele* reflects a world of magic, the artistic portrayal of experience in unity and illusion which more than a century earlier had been defined as Schiller's concept of play. But in Hesse the imagination as the highest union of opposites is viewed internally, as a transmutation of psychological experience into an aesthetic absolute.

III

Art embodies the union of dualities—of self and world and the projection of their conflict into the self—and portrays it in a state of "magic." This unity is found through an apprehension of forms, that is, of moments of unity envisioned within the contradictory flow of experience.

Unity, Hesse suggests in "Wagner," lends active form to the imagination (IV, 589). When unity has been achieved, art can take on the form of the imagination and sustain it through time. In other words, the artist can freeze the moments of reconciliation which in life are barely discernible in the ever-changing flux. In the aesthetic act, in which the self is opened up to the ideal world, unity is both the aim and the condition. *Siddhartha* exemplifies this point in spiritual terms. In this novel, Hesse speaks of the readiness of the soul to achieve unity by being able to think the idea of unity at any given moment within the stream of experience (III, 716, 720). To achieve this integration, a balance of illusion or detachment is necessary by which the true artist can reenact what is otherwise left to the inspired mystic.

The mystic achieves unity through his vision, but the artist attains it through the creative imagination. In *Guest at the Spa* (1925), written with Jean Paul's "Dr. Katzenberger's Journey" in mind (see Ball, p. 225), the self overcomes the hostile world, symbolized by the disagreeable Dutchman next door, through an imaginative act of will, which, while it is not "real" in a world of action, is nonetheless efficacious in creative illusion. In *Steppenwolf*, the conflict leaves the protagonist a shattered self precisely at the moment when resolution is imminent, because the hero cannot recognize and accept the truth of the aesthetic illusion and acts against the vision of his own integration by killing the image of Hermine. At several levels of the more complicated novel *The Glass Bead Game*, Knecht reconciles his internal and external conflicts through harmonizing visions which are often crystallized in aesthetic creations. Although the psychological motif has been largely translated into philosophical and mystical terms, the poems which Knecht composes in secrecy and the biographies which resolve inner conflicts in symbolic fiction both exist in the detached realm of art. Music, as we shall see, represents for *Castalia* the resolution of dissonances in aesthetic harmonies; the step beyond music in its hierarchy is the abstract Game of Glass Beads ordering contradictory elements of life in a universal system beyond life which the successful master controls.

The aesthetic imagination produces the sense that inner schisms can be bridged and integration found by the absorption, in illusion, of a divided or disordered world into a higher projection of the self. The dual nature of the aesthetic act as mystical integration and psychological dissolution and resolution, which is thus implied by Hesse, can also be found in Novalis. According to his *Fragments*, the absorption of the alien in the individual self through art involves a process of "romanticizing" through which a lower self is identified with a higher one. But, probably connected with this process, Novalis also speaks of another activity, the act of "magic," which is linked to the aesthetic mode of harmonizing. Magic is a merging of dissonances in harmonies; in individual experiences it may manifest itself as madness, but, if publicly exhibited and consciously applied according to rules, it becomes analogous to art.

Hesse is fond of the term *magic* and uses it freely to suggest both oneness in mystical experience and its sensible presentation in art.[16] The works of Novalis open for the reader a world of "magic" (*Betrachtungen*, p. 211). One of Hesse's essays on reading is called "Magic of the Book." Signs applicable to poetry are often called "magic signs." The poet, as "Childhood of the Magician" testifies, is occasionally called a magician.[17] Although as usual there is no fixed meaning attached to the term, its various functions seem to suggest the reflection of unity in aesthetic illusion, neutralizing the clash between the poetic sensibility and the hostile forces of the external world which it must seek to absorb.

Hesse's view of magic as a form of the imagination carries with it the intuitive meaning of vision or *Schau,* superseding temporal sequence and even verbal expression. The climax of "Summarized Biography," in which the author (an aging Socrates waiting for his hemlock in the nightmare of a Kafkaesque bureaucracy) climbs on the train of his own painting and disappears in a cloud of smoke, is an amusing example of the way in which Hesse has often seen the "dull consecutiveness" of time canceled out in a world of appearance and play. Narcissus and Goldmund differ, because Goldmund, the artist and child of nature, expresses himself sensually without words, while Narcissus, the intellect, lives by and through words (V, 49, 88, 286). The intellectual Haller dreams of a language which would "say the unsayable and represent the unrepresentable" (IV, 326). In "Bird," various interpretations of the bird's behavior are contrasted with the indestructible myth (symbolic of poetry) amenable only to visionary belief (IV, 542–545). Edmund's vision, in which the command to kill arises from the womb, is called up by the dreary teacher's discursive explications of ancient religions (IV, 513). Even the true genius of the Game of Glass Beads cannot learn his trade through words but must fathom intuitively its complicated mathematical and musical relationships.

Magic, as Hesse uses it, implies that the work of art is a reflection of

---

[16]In *The Glass Bead Game*, Hesse suggests that the "magic theater"—an obvious reference to *Steppenwolf*—represents the aim of the Game of Glass Beads; "magic" is harmony sought or attained beyond the "real" world. Hesse's view of magic calls to mind Novalis' "magic idealism."

[17]Objects of magic are withdrawn from the external world and incorporated into the self, to change not things but oneself (*Dichtungen*, IV, 451).

the self in a higher representation, canceling out its inherent oppositions in "appearance" or illusion caught concretely in the sensible object. Similarly, when Schelling referred to art as the representation of the Absolute in the original image, he stressed the prototype of experience which is then caught in the sensibly accessible medium created by the artist. Bettina von Arnim, with whose thought Hesse was well acquainted, echoed this view less pedantically: "Art is the evidence that the language of a higher world can be clearly understood in ours." Moreover, Hesse's demand that the artist's vision be whole and essentially nonverbal reflects an important aspect of romantic teaching which is epitomized in Jean Paul's comparison of the language of poetry to the language of flowers and in his suggestion that poetry must portray experience directly, transcending the time-bound, analytic world of philistines and pedants. As Bettina von Arnim proclaims in language rich with metaphor: "Art is also magic; it summons the spirit to a heightened visible phenomenon, and the spirit crosses the bridge of pain to within the magic circle." Hesse's narrative and descriptive techniques, frequently borrowed from romantic models, implement this view of magic in peculiarly modern terms.

IV

The moment of reconciliation must be frozen in time. To elicit "magic" from the materials of crude experience, Hesse must represent unity within the flow of time; the artist must capture the mystic's vision through his medium of words. This relationship between "dull consecutiveness" and the vision of integrating magic, particularly evident in the novel, had been thoroughly explored in romantic aesthetics. Novalis spoke of the novel as a "geometrical progression," the realization of an idea, an irrational magnitude, which can be demonstrated but not directly explained. In a similar way, many romantic definitions of the function of the novel relate progression in time to aesthetic reconciliation beyond time, which is required of the novel as prose discourse and as a form of poetic art.[18]

In practice, Hesse borrows a good deal from romantic sources, notably from Novalis, to portray the relation between the time-bound experiences which his protagonists encounter and their reflections in timeless art. Two motifs or methods, suggestive of *Heinrich von Ofterdingen*, have been used with particular frequency. The first of these is the

---

[18]*Dichtungen*, III, 364–383. The story "Lulu" (Lilia), inserted in *Hermann Lauscher*, also suggests Novalis' blue flower.

poetic symbol, the blue flower of poetry, through which the ideal above time can be portrayed simultaneously with a movement through time (the search). The fairy tale "Iris," for example, borrows from Novalis the description of Anselmus' search for a flower which represents mystical vision and, ultimately, art. In Hesse's postwar novels, specific symbols like the sparrow hawk and "Abraxas" in *Demian* or the flower symbolism of *Steppenwolf* portray reconciliations of opposites like light and dark, intellect and soul, unity and manifold beyond the time-bound order of the characters' lives. But as Hesse uses the "blue flower," the object of the poet's and hero's search often represents not only poetry but also a hoped-for or achieved resolution of schizophrenic states through which a torn self is raised to a condition of illusory magic. When Hesse claimed on one occasion that Jean Paul anticipated modern theories of the unconscious, he also revealed his personal conception of romantic attitudes, his own search for that bridge from conscious to unconscious experience across which he might reach resolution in spiritual and aesthetic harmony. Even in periods in which Hesse suppressed psychological meanings, he chose aesthetic symbols, like statues in *Narcissus and Goldmund* and *Journey to the East* or the Game of Glass Beads in *The Glass Bead Game* in which harmonies are achieved in the detached realm of a *play*, to represent a unification of dissonances "frozen" in time through sensibly or intuitively accessible representation.

The second method posits a wanderer through space and time who acts as a perceiving orbit, a passive protagonist in Novalis' definition, in whom encounters and dreams are focused and mirrored as art. Such a conception of the hero, which suggests a picaresque structure, is, of course, not confined to *Heinrich von Ofterdingen* but extends to many novels commonly associated with the romantic tradition, such as Goethe's *Wilhelm Meister's Journey,* Wackenroder and Tieck's *Franz Sternbalds Wanderings*, or Eichendorff's *Taugenichts*. Hesse poignantly utilizes the theme of wandering in *Der Novalis* (1907, published 1940), in which the structure and symbolism of *Heinrich von Ofterdingen* are suggested by a description of the transformations suffered by an old copy of Novalis' works. This story epitomizes the characteristic tension in Hesse's narratives between the world of images experienced in consecutive time and the sensibility of the experiencer which they ultimately portray. Moreover, as Hesse uses this method, the orbit of perception is turned inward. Like Wilhelm Meister and Heinrich von Ofterdingen, Goldmund and Haller wander through the world of sense and symbolic dream, their sensibilities modified by events and encounters. But Hesse, the twentieth-century novelist, dissects them more sharply. Unlike Wilhelm and Heinrich, Goldmund and Haller move through worlds which mirror, directly and allegorically, their internal states of mind, that is, disintegrations and resolutions occurring beneath the ordinary level of conscious and even unconscious experience. At the same time, the aesthetic purpose of Hesse's use of the wanderer from *Hermann Lauscher* to *Journey to the East* remains, as in his romantic models, that of portraying, within and beyond the time-bound world of sense, the moment of unified experience recognizable in art.

Music and painting are likewise effectively employed as motifs and literary devices to portray a union of opposites beyond time. In Hesse's reinterpretations of the romantic tradition, music functions as a combination of contradictory elements in self and world, either producing the dissonance of their continuous conflict which it is the artist's hopeless task to resolve, or harmonizing opposites in the "appearance" of art. In the famous passage from *Guest at the Spa,* Hesse dramatizes this point in terms of a significant personal longing:

> If I were a musician I could, without difficulty, write a two-part melody, a melody which consists of two lines, of two series of tones and notes, which reflect and enlarge upon each other, conflict with and limit each other, but in any case . . . at every point in the series maintain the most intimate, lively interaction and interrelationship. And anyone who can read music could read my double melody, could see and hear the countertone of every note, the brother, the enemy, the antipode. Now it is just this, this double-voiced and forever continuing antithesis, this double line, that I would like to express in my medium, with words, and I try until I am sore, and it still doesn't work. (IV, 113)

As a writer, Hesse longs to be a musician, not because he might feel more at home in a nonliterary *métier*, but because music embodies the very concept of harmony and dissonance which is his prevailing theme.[19] The clash of opposites and their reconciliation is not only heard and made visually apparent to the reader of musical notations; it is also dramatized. Each note is accompanied by its brother and enemy, its antipode. In this way each note catches moments of unity in a world where contrasts constantly shift, unite, and separate. In one sense this view of music takes on a psychological dimension as an expression of schizophrenia caught by the interplay of contrasting motifs in musical sound. But in another sense, the *Wechselwirkung* of the antipodes is reminiscent of Fichte's *Wissenschaftslehre* and especially of Schiller's dialectic of form and matter and their reconciliation in the *Schein* of art.

Music, therefore, suggests not only the harmony or dissonance of

[19]Curtius suggests that Hesse was more at home in painting and music than in literature (pp. 213–214).

opposing motifs but also the possibility of a "transcendental" albeit aesthetic solution. It is, in the phrase of Wackenroder and Tieck's *Fantasies about Art, for Friends of Art*, the only art form "which leads back to *the same* beautiful harmonies the most varied and conflicting stirrings of our souls." In *The Glass Bead Game*, music functions as a symbol for the resolution of dissonances. In this capacity, it organizes experience and directs it toward a total vision rather than toward its analytic and consecutive explication. As suggested by *The Old Music Master*, music is the means whereby law and freedom, servitude and domination can be combined (VI, 155–157). It thus implements the function of the imagination, which, in terms borrowed from Kant, acts as both the intermediary and the combining agent among opposing worlds of law (control and limitation) and freedom, yet which by its very nature maintains an illusory function. In this way music can be seen, with Bettina von Arnim, as the quintessence of imagination: "The infinite in the finite, the genius in every art, is music." Its language, composed of magic formulae, is apt to frighten away philistines as new and indefinable worlds are opened up. In his famous distinction of serious and light music,[20] and especially in his use of music in *Steppenwolf* and *The Glass Bead Game,* Hesse demonstrates the psychological and aesthetic importance of music as the prime mover of dissonance and harmony in life and art.

If music deepens the double melody of life and catches it in art, painting acts directly in halting experience, in freezing the aesthetic reflection in timeless portraiture. Hesse himself was a part-time painter, and in his fiction his own pursuit served to enhance his feeling of unity in illusion: the magic painting on the prison wall in "Summarized Biography." Diverse experiences, entire inner worlds, are gathered up in pictures or painterly images: the statues carved by Goldmund and the peep show sequences viewed by Haller. Sinclair in *Demian* portrays his own changes in successive drawings. Moreover, *Bild* as both image and picture leads us to link up the *Bilderwelt* of Goldmund's experience with actual scenic portraits. In each case, the inner world in which time is not necessarily a factor and the outer world which exists in time are both depicted in a way which lends itself to an instantaneous apprehension.

In Hesse's fiction, pictorial presentation is applied to narrative in two important ways. One significant usage is that of the idyll as suggested

---

[20]*Steppenwolf, Dichtungen,* IV, 402–403; *Das Glasperlenspiel (The Glass Bead Game), Dichtungen,* VI, 99–100. *Heitere Musik,* that of Mozart and Bach, represents unity in playful and detached clarity. *Rauschende Musik,* that of Wagner and Brahms, is found in the *Musik des Untergangs* of *Klingsor's Last Summer* and the music of the "Age of the Feuilleton" in *Das Glasperlenspiel;* it seeks unification by merging with the chaos of polyphonic life.

in Friedrich Schlegel's notion of the arabesque of *witziges Spielgemälde* and as applied by Jean Paul. In "Summarized Biography" the idyllic picture is humorously treated; in *Journey to Nuremberg* changing landscapes are often portrayed through the author's changing attitudes in the act of painting. Throughout Hesse's novels, stories, and fairy tales, idyllic moments and scenes occur as essential structural elements through which the hero's quest is accentuated and ultimately defined. But in another usage, as that of the self-portrait, painting has a further symbolic function. In *Heinrich von Ofterdingen*, the protagonist reads his own life as a book of pictures in the hermit's cave. In the same way, Hesse's protagonists, and occasionally the author himself, like Heinrich in Novalis' novel, depict their experiences so as to unify past, present, and future in a single moment of apprehension, of intuitive awareness of their own images. Perhaps the most poignant example of this method, extending Novalis' view of the interrelation of the arts, is the self-portrait drawn by the hero in *Klingsor's Last Summer*, which combines the effects of painting and music through a poetic description.

In the context of the narrative, Klingsor draws his self-portrait against a background of the "music of doom" which he hears as an accompaniment to his painting. This music frees Klingsor from a need to represent himself and his inner world naturalistically, because its harmonies and dissonances dissolve spatial forms. It liberates his vision so that the painting he creates is a self-portrait embodying less its object, his own image, than his inner dissolution within the context of a larger world. It leads him to modify the world as he perceives it and to absorb it into his imagination. At the same time that music releases the limitations of his painting, his painting acts to control the chaotic implications of the experience of music, setting spatial limits and distributions into which the musically inspired vision of intoxicated harmony can be placed. As a result, the painting is a double exposure of a limited self and an unlimited universe. It emerges as a work of imagination which expresses Hesse's view of the function of art as the heightened image of the self in which self and world are imposed upon one another in creative illusion.

> And he painted in this picture not only his face, nor his thousand faces, not merely his eyes and lips, the sorrowful canyon of the mouth, the cracked crags of the forehead, the rootlike hands, the twitching fingers, the disdain of the mind, the death behind the eyes. He painted, in his self-willed, overflowing, crowded and twitching brushstroke his life as well, his love, his faith, his despair.

This painting is not composed of the orderly sequence of pictures that Heinrich von Ofterdingen views in the hermit's cave. It is, rather, a condensed image of world and man, produced by a kind of "magic," in which seemingly disparate elements, landscapes and features, coalesce. This rationale of Klingsor's self-portrait also applies to other works. In *Narcissus and Goldmund*, different images are marshaled in the orderly sequence of allegorical progression, yet they are gathered up in the statues carved by Goldmund. In the Game of *The Glass Bead Game*, which can be seen simultaneously as musical harmony and abstract representation, distinct elements are condensed into a "picture" denuded of any visualizable aspects. Elsewhere, portraitures abound in Hesse's work, depicting the inner man as he absorbs an alien "world" and resolving the consequent conflict in timeless images.

V

Hesse's use of music and painting, as well as his employment of picaresque structures and unifying poetic symbols, is intended to implement, in modern terms, a romantic aesthetic turned inward. This effort arises, as we have seen, from a reinterpretation of a romantic concern with the "reconciliation of opposites" and of a corresponding view of imagination and art. Hesse's contrasts are sharper, more analytic in the modern sense, embodying a twentieth-century meaning of inner conflict, but they also retain the eclectic breadth of their romantic prototypes. For with all the accrued connotations of Taoism and Buddhism, of Freud and Jung, the essential conflict between self and world, intuition and intelligence, sense and intellect remains, with deepened psychological implications. These implications, however, have cast Hesse's romantic aesthetic in a distinctly contemporary mold, directly psychoanalytic in his work of the early twenties, rarefied by a search for more intellectually defined harmonies in the work of his old age. Indeed, the modern "inner" turn of Hesse's aesthetic, developing its rationale in more and more mystical and spiritual terms, represents less a departure into classicism than his most decisive achievement as a romantic writer in the twentieth century.

Murray B. Peppard

Notes on Hesse's Narrative Technique

This essay is intended as an introduction to the study of some salient features of Hermann Hesse's style. In order to have one central point of reference among the many works of Hesse, one short tale, "Edmund,"[1] has been chosen for detailed examination. From this one brief story lines will be drawn to many of the other works. In this way parallels may be drawn, comparisons made and differences demonstrated without becoming lost in the multiplicity of Hesse's works. One aspect of his narrative style that will receive some emphasis is the relation between theme and motif. Theme will be considered as subject matter or content, motif as the fictional invention or motivating plot force that sets the characters or ideas in motion. Hesse's major themes are relatively few in number and recur constantly in all of his works. His attitudes and his evaluations change over the span of his creative life, but his concern with a few topics remains constant. For this reason a study of almost any work from *Demian* on may be fruitful as a study of Hesse's main concerns in his writing; while the emphasis may vary, the subject matter proves to be remarkably consistent.

Before proceeding to a discussion of "Edmund," it should be pointed out that Hesse himself is the main subject of most of his writing. Some of his books, such as *Guest at the Spa* and *Journey to Nuremberg*, are straightforwardly about himself; in other books the confessional element is more indirect. In an essay written in 1928 Hesse says of his prose works: "In all of them the question is not one of stories, plots and suspense: rather they are at bottom monologues in which a single charac-

[1]"Traumfährte." *Neue Erzählungen und Märchen* (Zurich, 1945), pp. 165-176.

Reprinted from the Kentucky Foreign Language Quarterly, *vol. 6 (1959) by permission of the publisher. Quotations have been rendered into English by the editor.*

ter is observed in his relationships to the world and to his private self.''[2]
With this in mind it is not surprising that his fictional characters show
family resemblances. Mörike of *In the Pressel Garden House*(1920)
becomes Leo of *The Journey to the East* (1932) and Joseph Knecht of *The
Glass Bead Game* (1943). Waiblinger of the first book mentioned becomes Goldmund of *Narcissus and Goldmund* (1930) and later Designori
of *The Glass Bead Game*. Siddhartha of the book of that name is the ancestor of the music teacher of *The Glass Bead Game*, while Tergularius
of the latter book is an avatar of Hermann Lauscher and Klingsor.
Knulp's descendants are legion; all the wanderers and seekers that
follow are related to him. One might go back further and count the literary descendants of Peter Camenzind from the musician Kuhn of
Gertrud to the various persons in the collections *Neighbors* and *Byways*.
Klein of *Klein and Wagner* is related to Siddhartha by the final water
symbol at the conclusion of the stories concerned. The *Demian* theme
is continued in *Klein and Wagner,* in *Klingsor's Last Summer* and in
Narcissus and Goldmund in the sense that the intense search for the self
forms the basis of these books. But in the sense that a seeker learns to
serve and find himself in service for others, the line of descent from
Demian passes from Siddhartha, Narcissus, and Leo to Joseph Knecht.
Veraguth of *Rosshalde* (1914) is the literary predecessor of both Klingsor
and Klein. The H. H. of *The Journey to the East,* whose initials call for
no interpretation, is also an avatar of Knulp, but one who has read (or
written) *Demian, Steppenwolf* (1927) and *Narcissus and Goldmund*.
Many other genealogical relations could be shown, for the whole family
is quite evidently descended from Hermann Hesse.

For this reason the number of types portrayed and the relationships
into which they may enter are limited. Secular saints, seekers and sinners,
teachers and pupils, and sensitive youths with puberty problems are the
figures most frequently encountered in Hesse's writings. Lonely outsiders and wanderers on the path of life meet fellow seekers, become pupils
or teachers, learn about life and themselves and fulfill their fates. Even
the complex and enigmatic *The Glass Bead Game* may be viewed as part
of this general pattern. The germ of the book and the earliest parts written
are the autobiographies appended to the main body of the book. The
tendency to project one's own career into fictional characters and an
imaginary way of life finds its final form in Hesse in these autobiographies.

When we turn to the sketch "Edmund," we find a sort of dictionary
of the themes that are prominent in Hesse. None of these themes is carried
out and developed in full form; most are only hinted at or given a passing

---

[2]See *Das Werke von Hermann Hesse: Ein Brevier* (1952), p. 48.

reference in this little parable of education. An outline may be briefly given. At some time in the future, namely, the same time as the beginning of the "Summarized Biography" (1924), a period referred to by Hesse as coming just before the return of the Middle Ages, Edmund, for whom the story is named, is studying the philosophy of religion under a teacher called Professor Zerkel. Edmund is asserted to be typical of the younger generation of the time in his thirst for living spiritual values:

> What he sought to recognize and comprehend were the actual practices, exercises and formulas that directly affected life: the mystery of the power of symbols and sacraments, the techniques of mental concentration, the means of producing creative mental states.[3]

Professor Zerkel is described as being a representative of the older generation. He is a dry, skeptical, enlightened rationalist. Of him it is said: His interest in these studies was one of pure research. He collected and ordered these phenomena [i.e., religious documents] as another might collect insects."[4] In an advanced seminar with one other student, some recently rediscovered Hindu *Tantras* are being studied. The class translates a saying which deals with the healing power of meditation and concentration on one's inner self:

> If you find yourself in a situation where your soul becomes sick and forgets what is vital to itself, and you wish to perceive what it is that is lacking and how you may provide it, then make your heart empty, reduce your breathing to the very minimum, imagine the center of your head to be an empty hollow, direct your gaze to this hollow and concentrate on observing it. Then the hollow will suddenly cease to be empty and will show you an image of what your soul requires to go on living.[5]

While Zerkel and the other student discuss the passage from a philological standpoint and Zerkel sneers at it as propaganda advanced by the Hindus to keep the Bengalese quiet, Edmund follows the advice literally. A picture appears to him. He does not doubt the message, nor is he startled, but he feels that the image shows him the forgotten innermost need of his soul. In a sort of trance, obeying the inner command, he advances upon Zerkel and quietly throttles him to death. Edmund, in a state of euphoria, hardly hears the horrified words of the other student and leaves the seminar buoyed up by a new sense of freedom and vitality.

Even this brief summary shows that the action of the story represents

---

[3]"Traumfährte," p. 169.
[4]Ibid., pp. 169–170.
[5]Ibid., pp. 170–171.

but the sketchy illustration of a pedagogical imperative, namely, that one should let nothing stand in the way of one's education. Of the twelve pages, over half are an exposition of the cultural climate. This combination of criticism and psychological exposition is characteristic of much of Hesse's writing in the post-*Demian* period. Neither Edmund nor Professor Zerkel has any contours or any face, for they are merely names for attitudes. Certain attributes are ascribed to them during the course of the exposition which they then illustrate briefly in one or two pages. What we are told about them serves to characterize the age in which they are supposed to live, rather than their personalities. The satiric purpose of the description of this supposed age is obvious and reminds one not only of the "Summarized Biography" already referred to, but also of *Steppenwolf* and the opening section of *The Glass Bead Game*. The theme of the tale is cultural criticism; the plot or fable is invented casually and developed only enough to provide an example of the sort of thing which might occur in the setting described.

This manner of writing is, however, typical of many of Hesse's works. "Bird," for example, is told for the purpose of illustrating the need for a sense of wonder and magic. "Of the Steppenwolf" is intended to show that not everyone has the inner strength to be an outsider and write his own law tables. "Augustus" asks the question: "What is happiness?" and answers it: "To serve others." These stories are similar to "Edmund" in that they are mostly statements of a single theme with very little inventive power directed toward narrative. What happens, insofar as there is any plot or narrative element, is usually a faint fictional representation of the thesis of the story. The fact that the moral or thesis is often directly stated in expository form is indicative of the didactic purpose so dominant in Hesse. Once one has seen the essentially essayistic nature of some of his shorter stories it soon becomes apparent that the primacy of pedagogy extends to the larger works as well. The classroom situation which forms the basis of "Edmund" will recall immediately other learning situations in Hesse. The teacher-pupil relationship is fundamental to most of Hesse's works from *Demian* on and is the most important motivational device which he employs. It appears in many variations and in more or less direct form as the most fruitful motif in his works. The episodic form of *Demian, Siddhartha, Steppenwolf, The Journey to the East*, and to a less important degree *Narcissus and Goldmund*, is held together by the relation of the central character to a guide or series of guides. Several variations of this motif are possible. In our tale, "Edmund," for example, Professor Zerkel is a negative guide, that is, one who must be removed if spiritual progress is to be made. Similarly, though less violently, the Buddha in *Siddhartha* represents the type of the rejected mentor. A guide may be temporary and appropriate

only for a particular stage in the development of the hero, such as
Prätorius in *Demian* or Kamala in *Siddhartha*. Or the guide—usually the
older, wiser person of the pair, who is meant to be exemplary in his
conduct of life—may represent the complementary alter ego of the person
guided, as in the relation of Narcissus to Goldmund. The archetypical
learner-guide relationship is to be found in *Demian*. From Demian's
guidance of Sinclair to the "Biographies" of *The Glass Bead Game* the
basic pattern remains nearly constant.

In this characteristic one-to-one relationship the main problem is one
of communication. Words alone will not do; wise precepts will not help.
Perhaps the most important statement concerning the inadequacy of
precepts is the section of *Siddhartha* in which Siddhartha rejects the
teachings of the Buddha. The younger seeker, who is finding his way in
life through trial and error, learns from the older guide's way of living
more than from his words or advice. One teaches, according to Hesse, by
living in such a way that the essence of one's life wisdom is an inspiration
to the pupil. For this reason the most idealized figures that appear in
Hesse's pages are teachers who are very nearly secular saints. The most
sublime figure of this type is the venerable music teacher of *The Glass
Bead Game*, who has his predecessors in Demian, Vasudeva of *Siddhartha*, Pablo-Mozart of *Steppenwolf*, Narcissus, and Leo of *The Journey to the East*. The autobiographies at the end of *The Glass Bead Game*
may be understood as three variations of this principle. That the hero of
this novel ends his life as a tutor to a single boy has been frequently
pointed out and discussed. The stories in which this educational factor of
the devoted guide is missing are generally concerned with failures in life,
such as Klingsor in *Klingsor's Last Summer* or Klein of *Klein and
Wagner*. With the preceding in mind it is evident that "Edmund"
represents an extreme variation of the basic pattern, namely, an inversion
or perversion of the teaching-learning situation characteristic of Hesse.

Other typical themes that appear in "Edmund" either directly or
allusively are the love for Hindu lore, the spiritual hunger and quest of a
young seeker, the violence of the resolution, the thesis of cultural decay,
the urge for self-realization and violent self-assertion by any means, the
sense of heritage and the permanence of values accepted as norms (by the
Tantras), modern depth psychology, the need for meditation in order to
effect catharsis, the moment of enlightenment or awakening—all these are
present in this little tale. They are, to be sure, not fully realized in
narrative form in "Edmund," but their presence is indicative of Hesse's
abiding interest in them and a reminder that most of the characteristic
Hesse may be found in almost any work.

In two earlier stories Hesse has depicted a violent solution to difficult learning situations. The fragmentary *Berthold,* written 1907-8, has as its theme the problem of growing up in a small South German town. Berthold, the hero of the tale, becomes involved in error and sin, experiences all the pangs of adolescence within his soul, and finally commits murder in order to escape from the mess in which he finds himself. At this point the fragment breaks off. It is clear that Hesse's interest lies in the moment of resolution and in the internal torment that leads to the violent act of release. Berthold is without the intellectual or spiritual interests that are ascribed to Edmund, but he is patently a precursor not only of Edmund, but also of Harry Haller of *Steppenwolf,* and, in his sensuality, the Goldmund of *Narcissus and Goldmund.*

Early in the story Berthold believes that he has accidentally killed a playmate. Although he feels deep relief when he discovers that the playmate has not died, the incident is described by the author as being a significant one in his process of growing up and finding himself. Berthold is described as being hungry for knowledge. Although the author tells us that he is not clearly aware of it, he is, like Edmund, really seeking knowledge of his own inner self. When, at the end of the fragment, Berthold kills his supposed rival as a drastic solution to his state of emotional distress, he feels no remorse for this crime, but rather a sense of release and relief, and, like Edmund, looks forward confidently to a new life. The ethics of self-development and the violent solution of emotional problems are common to both stories, but in *Berthold* there is not yet the thought of spiritual regeneration, a theme which is central to Hesse's writing from *Demian* on. Tension within the framework of family discipline, adjustment to school discipline, and the temptations of sex are the means by which Hesse sets in motion the above themes. Family and school remain throughout Hesse's work the most important settings for the development of his heroes.

The curious little tale, "The Wood-Man," written in 1914, sketches briefly the beginning of the career of the young Kubu. It is placed in time at the dawn of man's rise from savagery. The hero Kubu has in his heart the dream of a bright, new world. He escapes from the oppressive gloom of the primeval forest and the dark, mysterious and bloody religion of the forest by killing the tribal priest. It is not a simple act of revenge or of hate, but is, like the murders in "Edmund" and *Berthold,* a means of release of inner powers and an escape from the bonds that fetter self-development. The priest represents the obstacle to the realization of the vision within Kubu. This obstacle must be removed. As in the other stories we have considered, the reader is left to imagine the further career of the person who has escaped. Kubu is not really a person with a fully drawn personality any more than is Berthold or Edmund. He is merely the bearer of the vision of a better world. The priest represents the reactionary force of unenlightened religion. The tale is a parable of cultural progress, just as "Edmund" is a parable of learning. Nothing described in the story and nothing told us about the actors is meant for its own sake, but is on the contrary intended to exemplify the thesis of the story. It is characteristic of Hesse that he takes the standpoint of the all-knowing author, ascribes certain attributes to the hero, tells us what he thinks and feels, and invents a situation which allows the hero to demonstrate these thoughts or feelings. Frequently the plot is a pale exemplification of the theme. Important for Hesse is the description of the emotional crisis and the moment of resolution. Only in *Klein and Wagner* does Hesse deal at length with the protagonist after the violent moment of release.

With *Demian* (1919) Hesse enters his second period of creativity and the time of his greatest concern with depth psychology. This book is also the first to set the basic narrative pattern which we have observed in "Edmund," namely, the combination of cultural criticism and inner spiritual development. This pattern, although varied and modulated, remains very nearly constant through *The Glass Bead Game*, Hesse's last major fictional work. The motif of the older, wiser guide also receives in *Demian* its classic formulation. The theme of the book is simple and is given at the outset: "I wanted to try to live according to nothing else but what came of itself from within me. Why was that so very difficult?" The problem of finding one's self and one's way in life is the dominant theme. The criticism of bourgeois life and standards forms the secondary theme. The first chapter, entitled "Two Worlds" reminds the reader of "A Child's Soul," is similar to the opening of "Summarized Biography" and contains echoes of *Hermann Lauscher*, but as the story progresses the tortured self-awareness and almost morbid introspection of the central character mark a new departure in Hesse's writing. From this period on the preoccupation with the inner life of the hero forms the substance of Hesse's writing.

This concentration on the inner life of the central figure leads to a breakdown of the formal structure of the novel. Since the main concern is the recording of subjective impressions and stages of inner growth, the form of the diary or the thinly disguised essay is immediately suggested. Plot and plot development become a noting of stations along the path of development. The reflective element, especially when the hero is so absorbed with himself, and the need for interweaving inner psychological processes with a critique of bourgeoise culture lead naturally to the form of the essay. The search for the self is at once both theme and motif. Every encounter which the hero has is there not for its own sake but as a means of illustrating a new stage of development and a different type of response. Our starting point, "Edmund," illustrates an isolated situation and the response to it. If several prior episodes from Edmund's adolescence were invented to precede it, one would be on the way to having a book such as *Demian*. There is no system of motifs to supply a narrative framework and little effort is made to give form and shape to an outer reality or to conjure up a world other than that which lies behind the walls of the hero's egocentricity. "World" is seen mainly as that which impinges, usually painfully, on the consciousness of the hero. The responses of the subject are the substance of the book; a précis of the plot in its essentials would list these responses.

It is not so much a question in Hesse of ordering one's universe and finding one's place in an objective reality as of taking "The Way Within" with all its depths and dangers. Knowledge of the self often seems to involve just that and nothing more; it does not necessarily result in placing one's self in the framework of a reality made up of other real objects or people, but rather leads to a mystique of an all-pervading ego which sees all in its own image or as a reflection of itself. For this reason Hesse makes frequent use of the mirror motif, notably in *Klingsor's Last Summer, Klein and Wagner,* and *Steppenwolf.* Another motif which Hesse has used to good effect is the merging of apparently distinct persons into one. With this device Hesse is able to express symbolically the tendency of the ego to absorb all that it experiences. Pablo-Mozart of *Steppenwolf* immediately comes to mind, as does the merging of the hero with Leo in *The Journey to the East.*

The form of pure confession would lead to the diary or to a kind of stream of consciousness writing. Some setting other than the psyche of the hero must be found for communicating validly to others the subjective stirrings and promptings of the ego. Perhaps for this reason Hesse developed as one of his major motifs the idea of the "Orders." This is in part a compensatory device. Sinclair and Demian dream of an order of like-minded spirits, but not until *The Journey to the East* and *The Glass Bead Game* did Hesse depict an order in such depth and detail that it became the basic framework of the story. The last-mentioned book is, in fact, an outgrowth of the Castalian Order and its game of glass beads. The game is the leitmotif of the book, and the order, which is a realm unto itself, holds the story in its frame as the basic motif of the book. An order, whether secular or religious, provides a sphere of activity and an opportunity to serve. Since the theme of service to one's fellow men becomes a major note from *Siddhartha* on, the motivational device of the order becomes more and more important in Hesse's works until it reaches its culmination in *The Glass Bead Game.*" At the time of *Demian* Hesse had not yet created this means of achieving an objective correlative for his themes. His concern in this book is to show the pain that comes with insight into one's self, the problems of sin and guilt complexes, and the necessity of suffering for maturity. His invention in regard to plot is directed toward creating obstacles for the hero to overcome. Objective reality is present only as a problem for inner development. Kromer, for example, is not portrayed as a person, but simply represents "the enemy." The university does not come alive as an institution, nor is it described at any length. What we are told is that Sinclair rejects it.

In *Siddhartha* Hesse has developed a motif that serves as an objective correlative. The river in the latter portion of the book symbolizes the goal for which Siddhartha is striving. The ideal of absorption of the selfish strivings of the ego into service for others, combined with a sense of the flux and flow of life, is very adequately represented by the river. Prior to this the motivational devices were the relations to various people: parents, companion, teachers of various kinds (the Buddha, Kamala, the rich merchant) and finally the son. All of these are finally rejected. The importance of a setting as a motivating forces is not confined to *Siddhartha*. In *Klein and Wagner* Italy becomes a symbol for an imaginary South, a place where the moral rigor of the North is lacking and where times flows with mystic force in a soft and gentle climate. It is a refuge at first, until Klein's human relations become unbearable again. The final symbol is that of the sea. The urge to lose the self in harmonious absorption into a larger entity had been satisfied in life by Siddhartha, who found at the bank of the river serenity and peace of soul. Klein merges himself with the sea and achieves unity with something other than the pain of individuation only in the moment of death.

One motif for expressing spiritual progress, which we have seen briefly in "Edmund" and that is important for many other stories, is the moment of awakening. In *Klein and Wagner* it is called "the hour of reversal and revelation," in *The Glass Bead Game* simply "awakening." *Klein and Wagner* starts as a flight from the self, continues as a quest for the self, and ends with the symbolic submersion of the self in the sea. This progression is expressed by describing successive moments of insight. In *The Glass Bead Game*, "awakening" becomes a leitmotif that accompanies the spiritual progress of the hero. It is Hesse's belief that one advances spiritually in large measure through moments of great intensity of insight, moments of special grace in which one awakens to a new understanding. The scenes in which Hesse describes the "awakening" of his hero bind together the incidents of the narrative. Usually the event that follows is prepared for by the moment of awakening. In *Klein and Wagner* the drastic act precedes the insight into the nature and necessity of the act and the rest of the story deals with Klein's awakening to himself. In *Siddhartha, Demian,* and *The Glass Bead Game* such precious moments are described usually as being the result of grace in meditation or as the gift of a mysterious and benign power of enlightenment.

Common to all of Hesse's stories from *Demian* on is the belief that such a moment of enlightenment will come in response to a deeply felt inner need. Only in "Edmund" is the process depicted in detail as something that can be induced by will and effort.

Perhaps for this reason there is an atmosphere of gentle irony surrounding the tale. Edmund's generation is described as eager to recapture the spiritual wealth of the past. But its quest is for formulas, for techniques and practices that will produce a calculated result. The anecdote in "Edmund" concerning the university lecturer who imitated Novalis—he desired to practice controlling the body through the powers of the soul—and succeeded in dying at an early age, like the admired poet, is told with an ironical tone. There is no doubt that Hesse sympathizes with Edmund and his spiritual hunger, but at the same time Hesse is smiling at him and at his efforts to discover spiritual values through formulas. Hesse's irony is of many kinds and remains an element of his style which has not yet been satisfactorily studied. In some stories ("Tragic," "Bird," "Of the Steppenwolf") it is so obvious and so biting that it needs no commentary. In general it may be noted that Hesse treats ironically all attempts to achieve spiritual experience in borrowed terms. In addition Hesse satirizes Edmund's wish to find not so much values as powers. In this way the author is also ridiculing his own times, for even where a genuine desire for the spiritualization of life exists, as it is said to exist in "Edmund," one is forced to undertake the task in the terms which the *Zeitgeist* provides. The story is in part about the lasting force of values which were once accepted, and the efficacy of the *Tantra* is intended as an illustration of this. In order to appreciate Hesse's intent, one needs to know that a *Tantra* represents rigidly formalized, ritualized Hindu lore. Most of Hesse's stories illustrate the rejection of such dogma and emphasize the necessity for the individual search, the seeking, through trial and error, of one's own way.

This is the theme of *Narcissus and Goldmund*. To set this theme in motion Hesse has invented a kind of timeless Middle Ages through which Goldmund wanders while Narcissus remains in a religious order. The framework of monastic life is sufficient for Narcissus, who represents mind or intellect. For Goldmund, a man of the soul, a different setting is necessary. Thematically the part of the book that deals with Goldmund, and that is the major portion, is little different from Hesse's previous works. The motif of wandering, a main motif in Hesse from *Knulp* on, and erotic encounters with willing women are the chief motivational devices that hold together the successive episodes. The charm of the book lies in the skill of the author in evoking the aumosphere of the past. Again, as in most of his stories we are told about the thoughts and emotions of the protagonists either through philosophical dialogue or in straightforward expository prose. In narrative technique it differs little from previous works.

In his last great novel, *The Glass Bead Game*, Hesse has created a whole cosmos within which the career of his hero may move. Thematically the novel is a summary of Hesse's concerns over the years, but without the frenzy of works like *Steppenwolf*. It is similar to previous works in that it begins with cultural criticism and continues with the story of the growth and development of a single individual. But now this criticism is prefaced to the description of a whole imaginary world in which the life of the hero may unfold. The world of Castalia, the game of glass beads, the fiction of the hierarchy within the "order," the opponent and complementary figure of Designori, the sense of the "other world," that is, the world of history beyond the confines of Castalia—all this amounts to a framework of motifs that expresses perfectly what Hesse wishes to communicate and is of sufficient magnitude and plasticity to sustain the philosophical elements of the book. As has already been pointed out, the setting—usually a school, a town in South Germany, the family, a friend or guide, the atmosphere of bourgeois culture—is one of the important motifs in Hesse, since it enables him to register the responses of the hero to his environment. In this last novel it is no longer necessary, as it was in *Demian* or *Siddhartha*, to state in expository form the successive stages of spiritual or intellectual growth of the hero. In this book alone the hero moves within a world that functions constantly as an objective correlative of the emotions and ideas expressed. Once the symbolism of the game of beads has been established in its full scope, a mere allusion to it suffices to conjure up a whole nexus of associations and ideas. If one accepts the basic fictional invention of the story, it does not matter that the world in which the hero moves is purely imaginary, artificial and Utopian.

In summary one can see that the themes listed earlier are expressed in a limited number of motifs. The themes found in "Edmund" turn out to be the basic subject matter of most of Hesse's writing since the First World War. The motifs through which they gain objective form and receive a fitting embodiment in narrative style remain until *The Glass Bead Game* very nearly constant. Hesse's inventiveness is directed toward variations and modulations of a small number of themes and motifs which may be found, either realized in narrative form or in allusive suggestion, in almost any work. The search of a lonely individual for his own true self and his appropriate way in life is the single, dominant theme of most of his writing. The sincerity of the search, the pathos of the problems and the intensity of the colors and tones he is able to evoke make his works convincing and moving. He is able to let shimmer through an attitude of love for man and awareness of God that keeps alive a faith in a brighter world and a consciousness of the ideals of the spirit. It is for the charm of the situations and episodes and the atmosphere—frenetic like *Steppenwolf* or idyllic like *Knulp*– that we treasure Hermann Hesse, not for his conquest in prose of any large section of our contemporary world or of what he so often refers to ironically as "so-called reality."

Leroy R. Shaw

Time and the Structure of Hermann Hesse's
Siddhartha

In 1911 Hermann Hesse set out upon a voyage to India, "to see," he tells us, "the sacred tree and snake (of Buddha) and to go back into that source of life where everything had begun and which signifies the Oneness [*Einheit*] of all phenomena."[1] The vagueness of these words, written some ten years after his return to Europe, testifies to Hesse's uncertainty concerning the exact nature of his quest. The unity or oneness he sought may have been nothing more than a resolution of the conflicts developing within his own personality; it may refer to a cultural and political harmony he had not been able to find in Europe during the years before the Great War; or it may simply reflect the longing of someone steeped in the German Romantic tradition for a feeling of identity between the self and the world about one. Whatever the purpose of his search, however, it is clear that India, and more specifically the philosophy of Buddhism, which were familiar to Hesse from boyhood through his grandfather's scholarly and missionary activities,[2] were supposed to contain the goal for which he was seeking.

The mission was a failure, not merely because Hesse found nothing to match his ideal, but because the motivation for it had already prejudiced his chances of finding what he sought. The voyage, Hesse confesses, had been an escape, an attempt to exchange one continent for

[1] Hermann Hesse, *Gesammelte Dichtungen*, Suhrkamp Verlag, Berlin, 1952, III, 806. Hereafter quotations from this edition will be given in parentheses within the text. Unless otherwise indicated, all quotations are from Vol. III.

[2] Dr. Hermann Gundert-Dubois, Hesse's maternal grandfather, was "one of the first pioneers of Pietism's mission in India" and became an accomplished linguist and scholar of Indian lore. See Hugo Ball, *Hermann Hesse, sein Leben und Werk*, Zürich, 1947, p. 5 ff., 168 ff.

Reprinted from Symposium, *vol. 11 (1957) by permission of the publisher.*

another and to replace immediate circumstances with a more remote, but no less limited, way of life. He had compromised the hope of universal oneness, therefore, by assuming it might be attained through sacrificing one portion of experience and through abjuring the responsibilities which had bound him to a present time and place.

The voyage to India convinced Hesse that oneness, whatever it was and wherever it existed, would produce a harmonious condition in which every contrast and all opposing forces had finally been resolved. Furthermore, it had become clear that the unity he desired did not reside in any particular philosophy or place, but that it belonged to ''a subterranean and timeless world of values and the spirit'' of which the visible marks of a civilization were only an external manifestation. Unity, in short resided only in the timeless. With this realization the problem of finding unity became, for Hesse, the problem of transcending the limitations imposed by the domain of time. He had to learn to accept the present, but with the knowledge that it was only the embodiment of an essence which time itself had no power to destroy.

Siddhartha (1922) is in part a testimony to this awareness, in part a vision of the manner in which Hesse thought his problem might be solved. India, and the way of Buddhism, are joined to his own experience in the story of a man who achieves unity and the timeless through the realization that search, and the attainment of search, are simultaneous realities of existence. In the discussion which follows I shall try to show how Hesse was able to communicate this vision through an intricate and remarkable welding of meaning and form. *Siddhartha* stands almost alone in modern German fiction as an example of a work in which the structure *is* the idea, the latter growing organically out of the former and not fully revealed until the last element of composition has been fitted into its proper place.

Siddhartha, young ''son of the Brahmans,''[3] is propelled by the same search, and has the same foreknowledge of the goal, as Hesse himself. In the opening chapter of the *novelle* he is pictured meditating upon the magic syllable OM, ''the word of words'' which stands for Perfection or the Perfected:

> OM ist Bogen, der Pfeil ist Seele,
> Das Brahman ist des Pfeiles Ziel.
> Das soll man unentwegt treffen. (621)
>
> (Om is the bow, the arrow is the soul,
> Brahman is the arrow's goal.
> That goal one should always meet.)

[3]Brahman, first of the four castes, whose members were originally priests with the primary duty of studying and teaching the Vedas, the sacred hymns of ''Divine Knowledge.'' Not to be confused with Brahma(n), the supreme soul of the universe.

OM, the alpha and omega of every Vedic text, is a symbol for that "holy power," as Heinrich Zimmer describes it, which "turns into and animates everything within the microcosm as well as in the outer world,"[4] a power without form or substance itself and yet the source of everything that was, is, or shall be. Brahman, the impersonal and universal godhead, is one aspect of this power, and Atman, the individual soul of Self, is an expression for the infinite aspects which are identical to it. To merge within this micro-macrocosmic essence, then, and by this merging find the unity which is without time and yet made manifest only in the multiplicities of time, is the goal Siddhartha envisages as the perfect fulfillment of his way upon earth.

The vocabulary of Indian philosophy suggests first of all the several dimensions concentrated in the single action of this *novelle*. Although Siddhartha's story recapitulates the search of a contemporary Westerner, it also recalls the hyperconscious striving of an immemorial Eastern tradition as well. "The search for a basic unity underlying the manifold of the universe," according to Zimmer, had been "the chief motivation" of Indian philosophies since the time of the earliest Vedic hymns.[5] *Siddhartha* is a legend, therefore, a story which is the amalgam of several possible actions, each of which has its origin in a discrete moment of historical time and yet is simultaneously identified with a multitude of other actions taking place on other levels of experience.

Legend as the framework of the *novelle* offers the first clue to the manner in which Hesse imagined the attainment of a timeless reality. A second is given in Siddhartha's unusual foreknowledge of the goal. Like Hesse's own yearning to "go back into the source of life," Siddhartha's undertaking bears the characteristic of a return to, or from another point of view, of a discovery, by the self, of something that is already there. In his own words, he seeks "at-homeness in Atman," a goal which is at the same time the place from which he has already departed. Unlike the classic novel of development, the story of Siddhartha's way to perfection is not the logical and inevitable unfolding of one event out of the other towards an end which could not have been foreseen from the beginning; it is rather an ever-expanding awareness of a reality already known, a progression which is at the same time a regression to a condition forever in being. We must be prepared, therefore, for a type of structure in which the various moments of the protagonist's life are presented as parts of a whole that is already existent even though it has not yet been realized in his actual experience. The events of the story occur in the fleeting instant, to be sure, but an instant in which the goal as well as the search, the

[4]Heinrich Zimmer, *Philosophies of India*, ed. Joseph Campbell, Bolingen Series XXVI, Pantheon Books, New York, 1951, p. 79.

[5]Ibid., p. 338.

process of what is developing as well as the end of development, are both implied.

With these facts in mind we may turn now to the implications of Hesse's title, with its suggestive reminder that the historical Buddha, Gotama Sakyamuni,[6] acclaimed during his own lifetime as One who had found the way to Perfection, himself bore the given name of Siddhartha. It is striking that the life of Hesse's protagonist runs almost parallel to the little that is known of the Buddha's obscure history. The latter involves three basic events: the leave-taking from his father's house, the frustrating years wasted in vacillation between the pursuit of worldly desires and a life of extreme asceticism, and finally, the determination of the Middle Path as the only road to Enlightenment. Siddhartha also follows this course, if not in strict chronological sequence, still in the same pattern of significant experiences. The sole difference here—which, as I shall try to show, amounts to only a superficial distinction—consists in the fact that the Buddha left a body of sermons and teachings which are not advanced by Hesse's hero.

The parallel just noted, which forms the structural backbone of this work, comes from Hesse's desire to superimpose upon his story of the seeker a portrait of the sage who had already found his way. Being and Becoming are both represented in the story, therefore, the former in the existence of a man who has found unity, the latter in the presence of a man who has identified himself with perfection although he is still approaching it. In this sense, time, the troubled present in which one seeks the way, is transcended in the *novelle* by the timeless fact of the goal already achieved. Siddhartha, indeed, is both seeker and sage, the One in whom perfection hovers as a silent attendant within the actions of the One who is still unperfected. His actual encounter with the Buddha in the course of the story anticipates this absolute crossing of the timeless with time, for here the aspect of life which is Becoming meets the aspect of a life already in Being, the One who is already perfect encounters himself in the process of attaining perfection. The fact that these two aspects do not coalesce at this point, and that Siddhartha refrains from declaring himself a disciple of Gotama although acknowledging the latter as a living Buddha, is essential to Hesse's message, for it signifies the distance which experience always intrudes between the seeker and his goal. Time, the sum of moments which the Buddha has already transcended in himself, must first be lived out in Siddhartha's own life.

The course of Siddhartha's discovery of the Self, his realization, so

[6]Siddhartha, "Desire accomplished," is the given name; Gotama or Gautama, the name by which Buddha is generally known and also the name of a great teacher and founder of the Nyaya system of philosophy; Sakyamuni means "Silent sage of the Sakyas," the clan to which Gotama belonged.

to speak, of the Buddha who is already within him, is therefore a process of acquiring the wisdom of the historical Sakyamuni while he himself is finding the way to enlightenment. The external design of the *novelle*—its division into two major parts, of which the first contains four, the second eight separate sections—corresponds in extremely subtle fashion to the Buddha's celebrated doctrine of the Four Noble Truths and the Eightfold Path to salvation from human suffering. This is not to say that *Siddhartha* is intended as a biography of the Buddha, or as a literal presentation of his doctrine, but that it has drawn upon the essential language of Buddhism in order to support Hesse's identification of the One-in-Being with the One-Becoming by tracing the seeker's acquisition of those virtues which are the special wisdom of an enlightened sage.

The first part of the *novelle*, written near the end of the First World War,[7] brings Siddhartha the knowledge of Buddha's Four Noble Truths. The experiences recounted here reflect certain events in Hesse's life up to his return from India and convey the realization, already noted, that the problem of finding unity was a problem of transcending time and that, paradoxically, the way into this timeless realm led through the multiple fields of the Here and Now. In the second part of the *novelle*, then, Siddhartha undertakes this journey through experience and arrives at the goal he is seeking.

Buddha's First Noble Truth is revealed to Siddhartha while he is still a son of the Brahmans dwelling in his father's house. The world of the father is a world of things as they have become, determined by the past and geared to the perpetual repetition of an unchanging way of life. Ritual and formula govern this world, and life in it revolves around the rendering of sacrifices and offerings at "the accustomed time," the performance of established duties from which not even the "most blameless" of men, Siddhartha's own father, is free. He must "cleanse himself every day, strive for purification every day, every day anew" (621).[8]

The world of the father, then, is fixed in the moment and regulated according to the set times of an inherited manner of existence. What will come is the same as what has been; the present exists only as the appointed moment for acting within a cycle of time that is forever revolving around the same course. This, Hesse indicates, is the world into

---

[7]The first part, up to the point where Siddhartha is found at the river by his friend Govinda, was written in the winter of 1919; the remainder was finished after a year and a half. Ball's *Hesse*, p. 169.

[8]A separate essay might be written on the splendid manner in which Hesse has managed to convey the rigidity of that world in his prose. Variations in style throughout the *novelle* correspond to the basic discoveries Siddhartha makes in each chapter, yet one never loses the feeling that the same person is involved in these various experiences and that they all belong to the same process.

which all men are born—orthodox, traditional, determined by the past—a world in which they suffer not only from the imposition of a way of life that is not of their own making, but also because time, the necessity of living according to a ritualized moment, stands between them and the reality they seek. Between Brahman and Atman, the universal godhead and the Self that is supposed to be identical to it, lies the ethic of the gods and their demands, mere formulas for life which are no less "ephemeral and subject to time" than man himself. Thus Siddhartha, as a son of the Brahmans, suffers from the impossibility of translating the consciousness of truth, his foreknowledge of the goal, into the actual experience of living free from the repeated phases of established time.

When he leaves this world of the father, Siddhartha sets out with his friend Govinda to find a place in which "the cycle of time might be eluded, the end of causes [found], and an eternity without suffering would begin" (627). Like the historical Buddha, he joins the jackal men called Samanas,[9] fanatic ascetics for whom enlightenment was to be found only through denial of the flesh and all worldly desires. Among the Samanas Siddhartha tries "to kill memory and his senses," to deny the sum of things as they had been, withdraw from the present, and close himself off from the possibility of further experience. He tries, in short, to escape from time. The arts of the Samanas are conscious attempts of the intellect, exercising itself through the will, to free the self from all temporal effects. Through fasting, Siddhartha tries to make himself physiologically independent of the moment; through thinking, to control what the moment might bring him and to determine his own attitude towards it; and through waiting, to suspend the moment between a part he has rejected and a future condition which he hopes to will into existence. The purpose of Siddhartha's life among the Samanas may be summed up in the rhyming words *leer* (empty) and *nicht mehr* (no more): to be no longer subject to the experience of time, but to be "empty of thirst, empty of desire, empty of dream, empty of joy and sorrow," to become a void which only Atman-Brahman, the timeless unity of his search, would be sufficient to fill.

The way of asceticism succeeds only in revealing to Siddhartha the second of Buddha's Noble Truths—that the cause of suffering is the craving for something which can never be satisfied: "Although Siddhartha fled from himself a thousand times, lingered in nothingness, in an animal, in a stone, the return was inevitable, the hour unavoidable when he came back to find himself once more, in moonlight or in sunshine, in shadow or in rain, when he became himself again, Siddhartha once more,

---

[9] Samana, "the equalizing breath," apparently Buddha's own name for the extreme ascetics and the life he had lived among them (see Kenneth J. Saunders, *Gotama Buddha*, New York, 1920, p. 23).

and again felt the torture of an imposed cycle of time'' (627–628). No matter what his way of escape, then, Siddhartha always returns to the self restricted by time. Thus he realizes not merely that asceticism can bring him no salvation, but also that it is impossible to solve the problem of time by trying to crush it with an act of will. His attempts to escape from suffering only lead to further suffering; the denial of the moment serves only to accelerate the temporal cycle. Siddhartha has learned that the timeless may not be found apart from the medium of that self which time is still in the process of making. Being does not reveal itself through the negation of Becoming.

In ''Gotama,'' the next chapter of the *novelle*, Siddhartha discovers the third of Buddha's Noble Truths through an encounter with the historical sage himself. The presence of the Enlightened One proves that there is a way of release from suffering. Gotama has made ''the highest wisdom his own; he has remembered his previous lives, he had reached Nirvana and returned no longer into the cycle of time, he immersed himself no longer in the murky stream of illusionary forms'' (632).[10] In Buddha, then, the searching Siddhartha sees a living demonstration of the fact that it is not necessary to depart from time in order to know the timeless. Yet at the same time the presence of the Buddha, who has learned to preserve the memory of what was and yet not be bound to it, who has found his place in the present and yet is still at home in Atman, is a reminder that the roots of the timeless are embedded in the experiences acted out within the world of time.

Siddhartha's recognition of Gotama is unhesitating and unequivocal: I have not doubted for a moment that you are Buddha, that you have reached the goal, the highest, which so many thousand Brahmans and sons of the Brahmans are looking for'' (642). Nevertheless, he does not become a disciple of Buddha, as his friend Govinda does, for reasons which are both pertinent and revealing. The Samanas had taught him to look upon experience only with his intellect; under this influence, he cannot overlook a logical error in the Buddha's teaching. Gotama, he claims, had clearly demonstrated ''the unity of the world, and the interconnection of all that happens,'' but he had himself broken that unity by advising one to overcome the world and seek salvation outside of it. In contradiction to his own presence, therefore, Gotama seems to Siddhartha to preach that timelessness lies in abjuration of the world and of present time.

[10]It is interesting to note that the rumors Siddhartha hears of Buddha are the same as those spread about Christ. Ball has pointed out the similarity between Hesse's portrait of Siddhartha and his portrait of St. Francis—a conscious attempt, perhaps, to suggest the timeless essence or harmony between the dissimilar figures of varying times and civilizations.

Buddha himself answers this argument in warning Siddhartha against a too zealous and trusting attention to words: ''Be on your guard, o eager seeker for knowledge, before the thicket of opinions and the strife over words'' (642). Buddha may speak this way, indeed, because he knows that wisdom is not limited to his own doctrine and because that doctrine has been promulgated solely for the sake of those, like Govinda, who depend upon another's word in order to receive a hint as to their own way into enlightenment. Eventually, when he has reached the wisdom the Buddha now possesses, Siddhartha will admit the justness of Gotama's admonition. ''Salvation and virtue, even Sansara and Nirvana,''[11] he will tell Govinda, ''are only words. There is no Nirvana as such; there is only the word'' (728).

Siddhartha refuses to become a disciple of Buddha for another reason which is more fundamental, perhaps, since it leads to a revelation of the fourth Buddhistic truth. ''One thing,'' he says to Gotama, ''is not contained in your clear and most respected doctrine; it does not contain the secret of what the Buddha has experienced himself'' (643). Buddha, in other words, cannot direct Siddhartha towards his goal because the way lies through Siddhartha's knowledge of himself. This is at one and the same time a confession that a man may not learn salvation from any teacher, even if that teacher be Buddha himself, and a recognition that the path to unity and the timeless lies through one's own experience of temporality, in that very process of Becoming which seems to contradict the absolute state of Being.

In ''Awakening'' Hesse stresses the word *hier* (here) as the sign of Siddhartha's acceptance of the fact that his way of discovery leads through the determining world of the Here and Now. After perceiving this truth, Siddhartha suddenly finds that ''the world is beautiful, the world is many-colored, the world is strange and full of mystery'': ''Here was blue, here was yellow, here was green. The sky was in flux, as was the river, the forest was silent, as were the mountains, everything was beautiful, everything mysterious and magical, and in the middle of it all was Siddhartha, the Awakening One, on the way to himself. . . . Meaning and essence were not hidden somewhere behind things; it was in them, in everything'' (647). Thus in the midst of what exists with himself as the center of the various phenomena in time, Siddhartha sets out to discover what he is. He calls this turning point in his life a rebirth, the first

[11]Opposite and key terms in Buddhistic teaching. Sansara is the ''round of being,'' transmigration in the cycles of time; Nirvana, ''blown out,'' is the state of enlightenment when the flame of temporal existence has been extinguished. Siddhartha's insistence that these are mere words is quite in keeping with the spirit of Buddhism. ''So long as nirvana is looked upon as something different from samsara [*sic*], the most elementary error about existence still has to be overcome'' (Zimmer's *Philosophies*, p. 481).

of several in the course of the action, a rebirth which signifies death to what he was and ignorance of what he is to be. He knows he cannot "go home any longer, no longer to his father, no longer back''; but he knows also that he does not know ''where he belongs, whose life he will share, what language he will speak'' (649). For Siddhartha it is a moment without a remembered past and without a discernible future, a present which is more than a time of transition, however, since it offers the potential reality of a timelessness that contains the sum, and yet is more than the sum, of all individual instants in time. Although Siddhartha barely realizes it, he is very close in this supreme awareness of a suspended present to the Oneness he seeks. At the end of a period in his life which had brought him the knowledge of Buddha's Four Noble Truths, he is ready now to enter upon the Eightfold Path, the way of multiple experience in time, which will bring him those virtues of enlightenment by means of which his Self will become at one with Brahman.

The first night after leaving Gotama, Siddhartha finds himself in the hut of a ferryman on the banks of a great river. It is an appropriate departure point for one who is about to embark on a discovery of the Self, not only because the river symbolizes the nature of the reality towards which Siddhartha is moving, but also because it marks out the course he must travel in order to arrive at the goal. Siddhartha will cross and recross the river many times during his error-laden search, and return in the end to the very place from which he started, with the realization that the several paths of his experience were all implicit in the beginning.

The river is the first of two master tropes into which Hesse concentrates the action and meaning of this latter portion of the *novelle*. The second is the image of sound, which Siddhartha first perceives as the innermost ''voice'' belonging to every object, by means of which it proclaims its own nature. As he contemplates the river, listening to it sing the song of itself through the forms and attributes peculiar to it, it seems to Siddhartha that the river is telling him how to undertake his own voyage of discovery. He must go the way of experience, getting to know himself in the course of creating himself, becoming acquainted with his own characteristics before he can find the nature of the being hiding within. In following his own ''voice,'' Siddhartha believes he has found the way which will lead him home again to Atman. ''He would long for nothing except what the voice commanded him to long for, linger nowhere except where the voice advised him'' (652).

Siddhartha's voice leads him first onto a path that is directly opposite to the way of a Samana. Instead of denying the senses, he decides now to exploit them; instead of escaping from the present, he elects to explore it to the full. With this decision he enters into that world of time which the

Indian pantheon assigns to the god Kama, lord of desires,[12] who has left his mark upon the names of those who are closest to Siddhartha during this phase of his life. In ''Kamala'' he becomes the disciple of a famous courtesan and learns from her the arts of love and sensual pleasure; in ''With the Child-People'' he is apprenticed to Kamaswami, a great merchant, and finds the secrets of success in business and commerce.

From both these worldlings Siddhartha learns much that is useful in the world of time: how to reside happily in the moment and induce it to yield its fruits; how to utilize the present so that it will produce a desired consequence in the future. Yet at the same time, and almost without his knowing it, Siddhartha's life in the world of Kama brings him the first of those virtues which are appropriate to a seeker on his way to enlightenment. From Kamala he learns ''right attitude,'' the correct way to approach an experience through complete surrender of the self even while the purpose of the experience is kept steadily in mind; and from Kamaswami he learns ''right aspiration,'' that there is no real profit in working for an immediate gain, as the merchant himself does, in constant fear of losing the little he already has, but that there is always a worthwhile return in any voluntary investment of the temporal moment.

The world of Kama does not, however, lead Siddhartha onto the way that is right for him alone. In learning from Kamala and Kamaswami, in following the direction they had taken before him, Siddhartha finds that he has lost his own path: ''going through the things of this world,'' he once tells Kamala, ''like a stone through water, without doing anything and without bestirring himself'' (663). He has begun, in short, to separate the Self from its experience, acting in such a way that he cannot become part of the immediate experience nor it a part of him. Gradually, then, as the years pass, Siddhartha notices that ''the divine voice in his own heart became a memory''; ''the sacred source which had once been so near and had once rustled so deep inside him was distant now and barely discernible'' (673). Thus Siddhartha learns, through his disappointment, the Buddhistic virtue of ''right speech,'' the lesson that one cannot hear the voice within if the ear is too closely attuned to the dialogue of others. He becomes like the bird which Kamala keeps in a golden cage: beautiful to look upon, but unable to sing, some day to be cast out upon the street to die.[13]

[12]Kama is discussed by Zimmer in a chapter called ''The Philosophies of Pleasure,'' p. 140 ff. The name does not occur in Hesse apart from its use in the proper names as I have noted.

[13]Hesse uses images very sparingly in *Siddhartha*; their beauty and appropriateness is therefore the more striking (cf. the image of the wheel of asceticism, III, 673). Much more typical of the *novelle* are the continuing appearances, either in person or in memory, of people who keep reminding Siddhartha of his search and his goal, e.g., Govinda, Gotama, and Vasudeva.

In "Sansara" Siddhartha experiences the last bitter consequences of a life adjusted to the sensuous moment. He finds that he has been playing a game "whose rules he endeavored to learn exactly, but whose meaning had never touched his heart" (666). And after becoming a perfect player of the game, as he had once been a model son of the Brahmans and paramount among the Samanas—the desire to excel never leaves this seeker for perfection—Siddhartha discovers that he has become a slave to the very thing he had mastered, a gambler, as Hesse pictures him, waiting anxiously upon every turn of the dice, hoping for a possible break within the cycle of predictable events. Even his play with Kamala fits now into this unending round of being, Sansara, "the game without end, a game for children, glorious to play once, twice, or even ten times perhaps, but [not] for always" (680).

In the end, Siddhartha's devotion to Kama brings him only the poignant experiences common to anyone who must live out his life in time. He encounters boredom, and with it the fatal necessity of repeating pleasures over and over in the futile attempt to keep boredom from returning. And finally, as the years accumulate upon him, Siddhartha sees that the cycle of the senses is revolving slowly but inevitably around the fixed point of death. One night, after a conversation in which Kamala begs him to tell again of his meeting with Gotama, Siddhartha "reads a frightened script underneath her eyes and near the corners of her mouth, a script of fine lines and soft furrows, a script which reminded him of autumn and of death" (677). Suddenly he becomes afraid, for the mention of Buddha, recalling him to his effort to free himself from the limitations of becoming, warns him that time is drawing to a close without his having found a way to transcend it. That very night, departing from Kamala's arms, he leaves the world of the exploited moment forever.

Siddhartha's renewed search for the goal soon leads him to the same river from which he had once started. Again it reflects his present state, appearing now as a boundary beyond which he cannot go, a literal reminder of the fact that he had exhausted the possibilities of search and still not found the essence for which he had been seeking. As a Samana he had emptied himself of all experience to create a void for the reception of Atman-Brahman; afterwards, among the childlike ones [*Kinder-menschen*], he had tried to accumulate experience in the hope that the sum of it would yield an ultimate reality. Thus frustrated at the extreme poles of time-denied and time-exploited, it seems to Siddhartha that there is nothing left for him to do and no place left in which to search.

Yet as he gazes upon the river, recalling the enthusiasm with which he had crossed it years before, Siddhartha remembers that the ferryman had predicted his return to this very spot: "Everything comes again, and you too, Siddhartha, will also come again" (653). The fulfillment of the prophecy comforts him, for he realizes that his life in the world of Kama was an inevitable, but temporary, phase of his discovery of the Self. The river represents not only the completion of one cycle of his existence, it marks the beginning of a new life with the past already behind him. Once more, then, as in the moment after his encounter with Gotama, Siddhartha is suspended between that which was and that which shall be, curiously close to the timeless because he exists in a present undetermined by specific time.

In this moment between life and death, Siddhartha falls into a deep sleep. And when, after several hours, he awakens, "the past seemed to him as if it were covered by a veil, infinitely far away, a matter of infinite indifference. He knew only that he had left his former life (which, at the first moment of consciousness, seemed far away like an embodiment, or an earlier existence, of his present Self), and that now. . . awake, he was looking out into the world as a new man" (684). This renewal through sleep, like Hesse's own descent into the underworld of the Jungian unconscious during the First World War, is not quite the same as the rebirth noted earlier in "Awakening." There Siddhartha had tried consciously and deliberately to break with the past, to deny what had been for the sake of what might come, exchanging one world of time for the other. The present rebirth, on the other hand, takes direct issue with the past and puts it in a proper relationship to present existence. As something once lived, the past is a matter of "indifference" and no longer has the power, as it had in the world of the father, to determine the future; but as a part of life, as a factor entering into the creation of what Siddhartha had become, the past, revealing itself through memory, exists still as a bridge between life experienced and life still being lived, a previous embodiment, in Siddhartha's words, of the present self.

The initial result of this dip into the past is to recall Siddhartha to his goal and to remind him of his continuing search. The sleep itself appears as a "long immersion in the depths of OM, in the Nameless, the Perfected" (684); and he awakens to find Govinda, the friend who had begun his search with him and is still seeking, at his side. With this recollection of what had been, this residue of the essential past establishing his permanent condition, Siddhartha is able to make a clear evaluation of the "round-about ways" of his life so far. He sees that it had been a mistake to try to control the direction of life, for this could be done only by submission to the repetitive cycles of time. "Your life is going backwards!" he tells himself, and considers that a long lifetime of experience and wandering has brought him nowhere at all. Yet once more the river, which mirrors his present condition in its constant flow downstream, also sends back the knowledge of himself by which his subsequent actions may be guided. In "At the River" Siddhartha learns the Buddhistic lesson of "right conduct," that one must take the way which comes naturally, heeding only the voice of oneself, without trying to arrange the course of discovery in advance. "No matter where my way will go," he promises, "let it go where it may, I will take it" (690).

The promise involves Siddhartha in a paradox, for he decides to stay by the river and learn from it, to find his Self, in short, by ceasing to create it through experience in time. With this decision the full significance of Hesse's choice of the river image becomes clear. In India, where water plays such a large role in domestic and religious life, and the cry of *Ko paraga?* (Who is going to the other shore?) is a familiar and often-heard phrase, the river has become a symbol common to all philosophies of timeless perfection. In the Vedic hymns the knowledge of enlightenment is called the "Transcendental Wisdom of the Far Bank," in Jainism the wise men are known as "Makers of the Crossing," and in Buddhism itself, the doctrine is identified as the "Knowledge that goes to the Other Shore." The river is life and the teachings of the sage are that "boat of virtues" in which the seeker undertakes his voyage to the state of enlightenment symbolized by the other shore.[14]

When Siddhartha decides to remain by the river and become a helper to the ferryman Vasudeva, then, he acts like the Indian novitiate surrendering himself, his own will and his own preconceptions, into the hands of a wise man in order to learn from his example how one may discover the way to perfection. Vasudeva (the name is that of a legendary Hindu king who was the father of Krishna, the Savior, and means "one who dwells in all beings") may be compared to the Bodhisattva of Mahayana Buddhism, "a sublimely indifferent, compassionate being who remains at the threshhold of Nirvana for the comfort and salvation of the world."[15] Because he has stopped at the brink of time and eternity, poised between this world and the state of enlightenment, yet with a knowledge of enlightenment, Vasudeva appears in the *novelle* as another aspect of Buddha, a sort of intermediary, let us say, between the aspect of Seeker personified in Siddhartha and the aspect of Perfected personified

---

[14]See the fascinating discussion in Zimmer, p. 474 ff. It should be remarked that the emphasis in Buddhism is on the crossing, not on reaching the other shore, for "Illumination means that the delusory distinction between the two shores of a worldly and a transcendental existence no longer holds. There *is* no stream of rebirths flowing between two separated shores: no samsara and no nirvana" (p. 479).

[15]Zimmer, p. 535. There are two Buddhistic traditions, the Hinayana, "little ferryboat," in which "the accomplishment of Buddhahood is regarded as a goal attained only by very few"; and the Mahayana, "great ferryboat," which teaches that the secret meaning and goal of the doctrine is the universal Buddhahood of *all* beings" (Zimmer, pp. 484–485).

in Gotama.[16] Vasudeva's function is to teach Siddhartha Buddha's "right means of livelihood," the occupation which, under the guidance of a maker of the crossing, will bring him knowledge of the virtues necessary for the final stages in his passage to the other shore.

The ferryman, counseling Siddhartha to hearken to the voice of the river, brings together the two main images of this second of the *novelle*: "The river has taught me how to listen, and you too will learn listening from it; the river knows everything and one can learn everything from it" (697). It is the doctrine that knowledge resides in the present time and place, and that from one's position in the Here and Now, in the depths of the fleeting instant, one can discover all there is to know. Wisdom lies not in denying the present, nor in trying to exploit it, but in accepting it as the repository for truths that are not apparent in the visible context of a single moment.

In his deep sleep on the banks of the river Siddhartha had discovered an unsuspected dimension to his life in the memory of a past which was still part of the present moment. In "The Ferryman," listening to the voice of the river, he sees further that his earlier distinction between past and present was only an apparent one. "The water ran and ran, forever and ever it ran, and yet was always there, was always and at all times the same and yet new in every moment" (694). Because it is "simultaneously here and there," no matter what its form, no matter what its position, "everywhere at the same time," the essence of the river remains always existent. And so it is with Siddhartha's own life, for he himself has always been the same in spite of the changing aspects of his temporal experience. Time, then, does not really exist: "Nothing was, nothing will be; everything is, everything has essence and is present" (698). Likewise, the experience of time—the fear of ephemerality, the weight of boredom, the terror of a determining past—are only the shadows of a mind thinking in temporal terms.

Without this fear of time, Siddhartha is soon able to destroy the illusion of multiplicity. As there are no breaks in his continual process of Becoming, of realizing the Being which lies eternally within him, so there are no barriers between the various phenomena of the world or between himself and these phenomena. The river, Siddhartha hears, speaks "with a thousand voices," all of them identical, the multitudinous voices of Atman echoing the single cosmic voice of Brahman. And the sound is OM, "the name that had always been and would always be, the voice of life itself, the voice of Being, of the eternal Becoming" (699).

Thus the difference between Siddhartha and Gotama, which had

---

[16] Another example of the three in one whose sum adds up to an invisible four (see below discussion on OM).

seemed so vast to the seeker at his meeting with the sage, becomes nonexistent. The knowledge Siddhartha has been acquiring is the same as that already possessed by Gotama, and in becoming enlightened, he has already begun to resemble the Enlightened One himself: "For a long time now [Siddhartha] had known that he was no longer separated from Gotama although he had not been able to accept his teaching. A true seeker, he knew, one who really wanted to find, could accept no teaching, but the man who had already found could approve every teaching, every way, every goal; nothing separated him any longer from the thousands of others who lived in the eternal and breathed the Divine" (701). So close is Siddhartha to this realization of his goal that Kamala, who chances upon him in her own search for Buddha, suffers no disappointment in having to die with only a glimpse of Siddhartha's face: "It was good, just as good, as if she had seen [the Buddha] himself" (704). Her death advises him of his nearness to the goal, if only because it confirms his knowledge that the final stroke of time, the cessation of temporal existence itself, cannot destroy the timeless unity present in all things. Looking upon her countenance in death, Siddhartha was "filled with the feeling of presentness and simultaneity, the feeling of eternity; in this hour, deeper than ever before, he perceived the indestructibility of each life, the eternity of every moment" (704).

If the *novelle* does not end with this awareness, it is because Siddhartha has not yet applied his wisdom to a situation beyond himself in which he is deeply involved. Up to now his problem has centered on the relationship to time as it has been experienced in his own life; he has not yet taken issue with what may be called the extensive future, that is, with that which will come after him and for which he is the specific cause; nor has he taken issue with the extensive past, that is, with that which has preceded him of which he is the immediate product. He has, in brief, not related his own Self with the uniqueness of the Self in others; he still needs to gain the knowledge of unity as it centers in experiences outside his own, in the lives of those who are linked to him through the accidents of time, and yet who must seek their own way into the timeless independently of him.

This final insight comes to Siddhartha through the son whom Kamala has borne him and whom she leaves in his keeping at her death. The boy arouses an emotion of which Kamala had accused him of being incapable: "Then, because his son was there, Siddhartha also became a childlike one, suffering because of a human being, lost in love, become a fool because of love" (710). His love is imperfect, however, because it is an attempt to imbue the boy, who has scarcely begun his experience in the world of time, with the knowledge the father has already acquired from his penetration into the timeless. Hoping to spare a loved one the suffering he has known, Siddhartha tries to make up for the son's lack of experience by giving him something of his own past, so that the boy may begin his life at the limits of his father's knowledge.

Siddhartha does not realize, as the boy does, that this is tantamount to making his son into his own image. And blinded by love, he does not heed Vasudeva's reminder that no one can determine the boy's calling, "to which way, to what deeds and to what sorrows" (707), since all must follow their own voice to enlightenment. Thus it happens that in becoming a father himself, trying to predict his son's life as his father had once tried to predict his, Siddhartha also becomes a representative of that world which is never acceptable to those who find it imposed upon them at their birth. The revolving cycle of time has described a full circle, therefore, and the truths of Buddha begin to reveal themselves again in the life of the son. Like his father before him, the young Siddhartha runs away to search for his own way into salvation.

With this Siddhartha learns the Buddhistic lesson of "right endeavor," that it is not possible to impose one's knowledge of the timeless upon one who is still subject to the limits of time. But he also learns that what he has experienced as a father is, in the all-encompassing circle of the timeless, the same as that which he had experienced years before as the son. Setting out one day to look for his son once more, Siddhartha pauses for awhile beside the river and there, as a reflection of himself, he sees the image of his own father, subjected to the same trial that he is now undergoing. This vision of the Self, posed in a situation of the past which had once been future, the image of a father-son dissolving again into the image of a son-father, proves to Siddhartha that the present moment truly contains all time, for it concentrates experience which, in the cycles of merely temporal existence, it would take several lifetimes to go through. With this realization, the limits to his previous grasp of unity are broken, for in addition to the knowledge which is already his own, that he himself is always the same in spite of a multitude of changes in his own life, he now has the knowledge that he is the same as all others although each has an identity of his own.

In "OM" the two master tropes of the *novelle* meet and mingle once more in a magnificent symbol for Siddhartha's final meditation upon unity and the timeless. The voice of the river, collecting the multitudinous sounds of Atman, the voice within each individual thing, becomes the imperishable and divine tone of all existence.

As in the case of the river, the full significance of Hesse's image can only be understood with reference to Indian philosophy. The sound OM, which accompanies every Vedic text, is perceptible either in the depths of Atman, the individual Self or soul, or in the world of Brahman, the universal godhead—in the microcosm as well as the macrocosm, therefore, joining the individual with the great totality of which he is a part, demonstrating that ''the phenomenal visible sphere (that of change, the Heraclitean flux), wherein the manifestations of time appear and perish'' is identical to ''the transcendent, timeless sphere, which is beyond yet at one with it (that of imperishable being).''[17]

Both timelessness within time and unity through multiplicity are represented by the traditional manner in which OM is uttered. In Sanskrit the first vowel of the charm is pronounced A-U; thus instead of two sounds, there are actually three. The charm is made by opening and closing the lips in movement from the back, open sound A, through the half-open, half-closed sound U, to the front closure of M.[18] One repeats this without stopping. It is, therefore, a continuous utterance, a circle without end, or a constant process of becoming in time in which the entirety, never wholly contained in any one part, is forever and timelessly existent. This invisible unity is symbolized by a fourth factor, or ''silence,'' obvious when the mouth is poised between final M and initial A, a silence which is considered part of the magic formula's total sound and is analogous to ''the silence always present in the creations, manifestations and dissolutions of the universe.'' Out of the visible three, then, is revealed an invisible four which is the essence of the whole, the being and unity underlying the becoming and multiplicity of the various parts. ''What has become, what is becoming, and what will become—verily, all of this is the sound OM. And what is beyond these three states of the world of time—that too, verily, is the sound OM.''[19]

Siddhartha's meditation in ''OM,'' the ''right meditation'' of Buddha's Eightfold Path, proceeds according to this mystic awareness. As he looks into the river, he sees a succession of images: of his father, himself, and his son, all of them discrete persons, and yet himself as all three; present in this moment are all the apparent stages of temporal succession. Similarly, the river sings to him three songs: a song of sorrow, a song of longing, and a song of joy, each of them different, each of them distinct historically in terms of its appearance in Siddhartha's own life, but all of which are present in him and are included in that great ''music of life'' implicit in every song and yet greater than any one of them.[20]

[17]Zimmer, p. 372.

[18]Each of the letters corresponds to a part of the Self: A is Vaisvanara, ''common to all men,'' the waking state; U is Taijasa, ''the shining one'' whose field is the dream; and M is Prajna, ''the knower,'' deep sleep (Zimmer, p. 377).

[19]Zimmer, p. 372.

[20]Ball (p, 175) has commented that the ''music of India'' in *Siddhartha* is a ''hieratic triad which makes the individual sentence resound like a constellation,'' but he seems unaware of the implications pointed out here.

"Govinda," the final chapter of the *novelle*, is a paean of "right rapture," the Enlightened One rejoicing in his enlightenment and yet mocking the glory of his knowledge by his admission that it is impossible to communicate it fully. In Siddhartha's conversation with his friend one can hear Buddha's warning that wisdom does not reside in the doctrine, that beyond the word lies the mystery, the silence out of which the sounds have come and into which they inevitably return.[21] Although trying to define the Being which is in and around him, Siddhartha knows that words are one-sided, robbing truth of its impartiality, emphasizing the rightness of one point of view at the expense of an opposite which is no less true. It is because this is so that Siddhartha cautions Govinda against believing in time, for "if time isn't real, then the span which seems to exist between the world and eternity, between sorrow and blessedness, between good and bad, is also a deception" (725).

As he reviews his life for Govinda, Siddhartha reflects that *einst*, the powerful adverb by which men try to distinguish between past and future, marks no real division in the fundamental oneness of their lives. It is a mistake to think of oneself as on the way to enlightenment, in the sense of progressing by stages in which one leaves off one thing as one acquires another, for enlightenment exists within one at every moment of present time. "In every sinner there is, now and today, the future Buddha; his future is all already there, in him, in you, in everyone there is the becoming, potential, hidden Buddha" (726). Similarly, unity, whether within or outside oneself, is not to be attained by trying to put it together as one would a puzzle out of many pieces, for it is present and entire in every object. Thus Brahman, the holy power identical with the Self, the timeless unity of all creation, is simply the reality discovered by lifting the deceptive veil of time as it is experienced in one's own life. Unity resides in the readiness, at each individual moment of time, to see the timelessness beneath, "to see all that has been, life being and life becoming, as simultaneously existent" (726).

In the last paragraphs of the *novelle* Govinda, the everlasting disciple and uncomprehending seeker, has a vision of this truth as he looks into the face of his friend:

He no longer saw Siddhartha's face, he saw instead other faces, many faces, a long series, a streaming river of faces, hundreds and thousands, all of which came and went and yet seemed to be there all at the same time, all of them changing continually and renewing themselves, and yet which were all Siddhartha. . . . And thus Govinda saw that this smiling mask, this smiling

[21]It is important to understand that in Buddhism final knowledge involves not only the destruction of all dualism (including the primary spheres of Sansara and Nirvana), but complete incommunicability of the absolute state of enlightenment itself.

of unity within the streaming forms, this smiling of simultaneity within the thousand births and deaths, this smiling of Siddhartha was exactly the same, was exactly identical to the quiet, delicate, impenetrable, perhaps good-natured, perhaps mocking, wise, thousandfold smile of Gotama, the Buddha. (732)

Thus the goal Siddhartha has realized for himself, the destruction of multiple time, is imaged for Govinda in the face of a living Buddha. And with this we too, who have attended the search like Govinda without a full knowledge of its implications, arrive at the wisdom which Hesse has made manifest through the unique form of eternal Being discovering itself in the process of Becoming. There is after all no difference between seeker and sage, no difference between Siddhartha and Gotama, no disunity possible for the Enlightened One who has found his way to the wisdom of the other shore.

Stephen Koch

Prophet of Youth: Hermann Hesse's
Narcissus and Goldmund

In every college of the land, the Hesse boom has hit peak phase and become so powerful that it has even knocked Camus off his ''portable pedestal.'' Ever since Timothy Leary pronounced *Steppenwolf* his favorite work of literature, Hesse has been standard psychedelic equipment, along with water pipes, day-glow art, the Maharishi, Jim Morrison and the *I Ching.* There is even a new electronic rock group on the West Coast called Steppenwolf.

Guruhood is nothing new for Hesse—I know Germans in their middle sixties who devoured each new book during their own adenoidal phase—and the role fits him rather well. His art springs from an unshakably profound infatuation with adolescence, and his vision of youth is underwritten by his incapacity to break loose from youth's fascination. His only interesting material is the passions of 25 and under: the pangy vertigo of limitless prospects, or the utterly pure, corny tenderness of narcissism, or the wild thrill of discovering feelings that are entirely new, *never* felt before. When he turns to other materials—as he does in the inexpressibly boring final two-thirds of *The Bead Game,* he can be a fusty drag, with all his limitations showing.

Like everything else in his work, Hesse's thought is irretrievably adolescent, so that in his chosen role of artist of ideas, he is invariably second-rate, although unlike the other prophets of the New Age, he is never *less* than second-rate. His thought is never cheap, never trashy, but neither is it ever intellectually exalting, the way the professorial, unfashionable Mann so often is. Almost without exception, Hesse's ideas are derivative, schoolboyish, traditional to the point of being academic,

Reprinted from The New Republic, *July 13, 1968, pp. 23–26, by permission of the publisher.*

influenced by all the right people, and boringly correct. Life, for example, is divided into Many Dualisms which cause Much Unhappiness. There is Intellect versus Passion; Thought versus the Senses; Good versus Evil; Self versus All; Male versus Female; Yin versus Yang. It is a Terrific Experience to Transcend these Dualisms and Make them Fuse. Likewise, the Self is limiting; it is a Terrific Experience to surrender the Self and confront the All. The Intellect is inhibiting, so it's a Terrific Experience to forget your brain and let the Senses take over. Good and Evil are all mixed up together, but they are both Terrific Experiences. The All is wonderful. Each of us has a Steppenwolf inside. The World-Soul is androgyne. Sex can be *wild*.

So, it goes, book after book, the Great Ideas chasing the Terrific Experiences home to their all-to-obvious destinations. Flawed though it sometimes is, Hesse's aesthetic sense is different and better than this; *it* does sometimes rise to extraordinary levels, does transform itself into ''something else,'' as the kids say. The final third of *Steppenwolf* is one of the great moments in modern literature, a moment original to the point of being in a class by itself, and one with an importance to future art which is not to be patronized.

This disparity between his intellectual and aesthetic capacities is one of the most noticeable facts about Hesse, one of those boring dualisms with which he himself was afflicted. It is this dualism which is the subject of the newly translated *Narcissus and Goldmund,* the medieval romance Hesse wrote just after he finished *Steppenwolf.* Like *Siddhartha, Narcissus and Goldmund* is not set in the remote past, though in this case not in Gautama's India but in medieval Germany. It is about the Artist versus the Intellectual. The intellectual in question is a monk named—what else?—Narcissus, and the artist is his pupil, Goldmund, as sensuously passionate as his teacher is analytic and cold. They thus make an all-too-perfect pair. In a fit of adolescent piety, Goldmund has decided to follow his frigid, beautiful mentor into a life of asceticism until the brilliant, sterile Narcissus perceives that his pupil's Tao, his ''thing,'' is a creative lust for the female. At this moment, the book reaches an almost grotesque symmetry:

> ''Why yes,'' Narcissus continued, ''Natures of your kind, with strong, delicate senses, the soul-oriented, the dreamers, poets, lovers are almost always superior to us creatures of the mind. You take your being from your mothers. You live fully. . . . You are in danger of drowning in the world of the senses; ours is the danger of suffocating in an airless void. You are an artist; I am a thinker. You sleep at the mother's breast; I wake in the desert. For me the sun shines; for you the moon and stars. Your dreams are of girls; mine of boys.''

"Your dreams are of girls; mine of boys." This sentence tears the heart from the mystery of *Narcissus and Goldmund*, because this novel is not really about the Artist versus the Intellectual at all. It is about wanting women. Escaping the all-male environment of the monastery, Goldmund embarks on his career of screwing girls, and *that* is the substance of the book. Lise, Marie, Lydia, Rebeckah, Lene, Lisbeth—Goldmund finds women everywhere, in every castle and field and town. There is a woman on every page, and every one of them loves Goldmund. The book is thus a strangely unsalacious but blissful male idyll. If *Siddhartha* is a cool canticle raised to the ideal of Ego Transcendence, *Narcissus and Goldmund* is a jangling rage in praise of heterosexuality. Goldmund is defined and created through women, who are the substance from which he derives his reality. They are his air; he breathes and devours them. And he creates through them.

Goldmund becomes a sculptor. He riots through his existence, leaving behind him a trail of girls, in Eliot's phrase, "sore but satisfied." He sees the face of the Madonna. He grows old. At the end of the novel, the aging prodigal returns to the monastery, where Narcissus, also aging, is still sterile, intellectual, and secretly queer. After one last fling, Goldmund dies:

> And now the sick man opened his eyes again . . . and with a sudden movement, as though he were trying to shake his head, he whispered: "but how will you die when your time comes, Narcissus, since you have no mother? Without a mother, one cannot love. Without a mother, one cannot die."
>
> What he murmured after that could not be understood. Those last two days Narcissus sat by his bed day and night, watching his life ebb away. Goldmund's last words burned like fire in his heart.

Even gossipy America has kept surprisingly well the open secret that throughout his life, Hesse was an overt homosexual. (The standard English biography by Ernst Rose doesn't give the slightest hint.) That fact casts another strange light on this book about woman-lust, and on the final destitution of its "intellectual"—the narcissist whose dream is of boys. It was surely as Narcissus that Hesse saw himself—mentor to youth, using his wisdom to liberate their sensuous creativity and thereby forcing them beyond him.

In 1916, Hesse was analyzed by a pupil of Jung—he was thus, so far as I know, the first major artist ever to be analyzed—and he surely accepted the Jungian message about maternity and death which he puts into the dying sculptors's mouth. The novel's last cliché about words burning like fire is too weak to suggest the obvious fact that *Narcissus and Goldmund* is not only about Goldmund's ebullience, but also about Narcissus' despair.

That despair is never felt within the dualistic structure of the book. True enough, one does feel Narcissus fighting his impulse to fall in love with Goldmund, and senses him inverting those impulses into thought. But the Narcissus-Goldmund syzygy is by and large maintained by a coolly symmetrical, organizational principle which makes the book's structure Narcissus-like while the details are Goldmund-esque in their sensuous, "psychedelic" richness. (An "oceanic" richness often awash in oceanic cliché, not terribly far from the prose of the *East Village Other*: "Suddenly in the middle of a page, he'd sink back into himself and forget everything, listening only to the rivers and voices inside himself, while they drew him away into deep wells filled with dark melodies." etc., etc.) Such a nifty paradox overlooks the fact that the book's best moments are neither "intellectual" nor especially womanizing, but are blasted with cold chaos. Goldmund stabs a murderous highwayman to death. He wanders across the terrain of the plague; he walks into a musty house where the dead family is still sitting in its chairs. He stumbles onto the corpse of a little boy, its tiny fists clenched in rage.

Hesse's habitual dualism is trivial academic rubbish: rubbish derived from a truth, perhaps, but still rubbish. Wittgenstein, it is said, aestheticized philosophy; Proust philosophized aesthetics. Both were homosexual, and so what? Nothing, except the obvious platitude—which is *this* book's obvious destination—that Narcissus and Goldmund and all they stand for are all mixed up together, bound together in their opposition.

But despite his faults, Hesse is a graceful and generally unpretentious artist. What can be said about his current bondage in the hands of the hippie philistines? A large part of Hesse's huge new audience reads nothing *but* Hesse, preferring nonliterary means for most of its Journeys to the East. It is an immense, energetic and ignorant audience with a wild capacity to co-opt the creative energy of high art (look, for example, at the way rock has swallowed in one avid gulp the whole ethos of "serious music"), and its charm and energy seem so vast that it repeatedly seems on the verge of subduing unto itself the whole world of making and emotion.

This capacity for cultural co-option scares the hell out of a lot of people, myself sometimes included. American culture is at the point of turning into a vast Children's Crusade, and Hesse is actually one of the best of its leaders. He should thus be discussed not only as an artist, but as a teacher. I shudder at what he would think if he knew how many in his audience think *Steppenwolf* expresses the view that Mozart "and all that stuff'' should drop dead. And yet, to turn to Orientalism and mysticism which Hesse feeds, though it is clearly dilettantish, naïve, and often damnably vulgar, I don't despair that some of the new *chinoiserie* may play some part in lifting the culture to a new stage of growth.

In *Steppenwolf*, Harry Haller—that poor, up-tight nineteen-year-old in drag as a middle-aged man—steps into Pablo's magic theater and discovers his own irresponsible youth. I sometimes think that at the moment, not Harry but American culture is reeling through the Magic Theater, rediscovering its own narcissistic youth in the midst of un-earned Dionysian opulence. The new, arrogant *embarras de richesses* of what is happening now is, undeniably, a liberation. It may even be a healthful one. Who can deny that the culture is almost screaming for re-creation or deny that the job will have to be done by people from that vast generation with everything on its side except that ''intellect'' which Hesse misrepresents in *Narcissus and Goldmund*. For the hippies are absolutely right: we *are* at a critical moment in the history of culture; we *have* been brought to a point of no return. But they don't see the intel-lectual challenge implicit in that fact, nor that the prime question is whether anyone can rise to it. I don't see any evidence that anyone can. Certainly, Hesse can't, and he is the most intelligent of the new doyens. But this ultimate sensitive schoolboy—this Compleat Guru—is never going to make it. The problem is bigger than he is: it is Nietzchean in its demands, and until minds that can cope with *that* begin to emerge—and in numbers—our famous Liberation is likely to remain stuck in the noisy, futile vitality whose source is neither chaos nor lust, but childishness.

Theodore Ziolkowski

Hermann Hesse's Steppenwolf: *A Sonata in Prose*

The critical and popular reception of Hesse's *Steppenwolf*, when it appeared in 1927, was so hostile that the author felt himself obliged to defend his book a good many times in letters to friends and readers. Again and again he protested that the novel is in no way a betrayal of the positive values which he had always expounded in his life and works, and he pointed out repeatedly that the book achieves a structural perfection which equals, if not surpasses, that of his other works.

Subsequent scholarship has substantiated Hesse's contention that the novel fits organically into the entire pattern of his thought and that it does not represent a defection from his earlier beliefs. But little or nothing has been done to demonstrate that his insistence upon the structural quality of the book is valid.

Among the many passages in which Hesse remonstrates against the criticism of formlessness in the novel, the following is one of the most interesting: "Purely artistically *Steppenwolf* is at least as good as *Goldmund*; it is structured around the intermezzo of the Tract as strictly and rigidly as a sonata and develops its theme purely."[1]

The present analysis of the structure of the novel can begin with Hesse's own analogy of the sonata, but for the moment it will be permissible to regard this analogy simply as a symbol of strict form in

[1]Hermann Hesse, *Briefe* (Berlin, 1951), p. 34; or *Gesammelte Schriften* (Suhrkamp Verlag, 1957), VII, 495—hereafter cited as *GS*.

Reprinted from Modern Language Quarterly, *vol. 19 (1958) by permission of the publisher and the author. A later version of this article appears as Chapter 9 in Professor Ziolkowski's book,* The Novels of Hermann Hesse: A Study in Theme and Structure *(Princeton University Press, 1965). Quotations have been rendered into English by the editor, and some footnotes have been omitted.*

general. It will be our task to discover whether and, if so, precisely in what way Hesse was justified in comparing his novel to a form which represents the highest in musical structure.

I

Confusing upon first perusal is the apparent lack of external structure in *Steppenwolf*: for instance, the absence of the customary division into parts and chapters. Instead, we are presented with a running record of a phantasmagoria of events, interrupted toward the beginning by an apparently incongruous document called "The Tract of the Steppenwolf" and introduced by the remarks of a minor figure who appears in the story itself. But if we look for internal structure, we see that the book falls naturally into three main sections: the preliminary material, the action, and the so-called magic theater.

The preliminary material, in turn, has three subdivisions: the introduction, the opening passages of the book itself, and the "Tract." These three subdivisions are not involved directly in the action or plot of the novel; they are all introductory in nature. This fact distinguishes them from the second and longest part of the book, which tells the story and which alone of the three main sections has a form analogous to the structure of the conventional novel. It relates action covering roughly a month, and it is essentially a straightforward narrative. The third section, finally, sets itself apart from the bulk of the novel by virtue of its fantastic elements: it belongs, properly speaking, to the action of the novel, for it depicts a situation which takes place in the early hours of the day following the final scene of the plot, and there is no technical division whatsoever. But the conscious divorce from all reality separates this section from the realistic narrative of the second part.

Beginning with this rough outline, we can proceed to bring some order into the work. The introduction is written by a young man who is revealed as a typical bourgeois both by his own words and by the brief mention he receives in the book itself. The function of this introduction is twofold: to explain the circumstances regarding the publication of the book and to portray the central figure through the eyes of a typical "Bürger." The young man is the nephew of the lady from whom a certain Harry Haller rents an apartment upon his arrival in the (unnamed) city. The date of Haller's arrival in the house is given as several years prior to the writing of the introduction, and it is stated that Haller lived in the house for nine or ten months. For the most part the strange tenant lived quietly in his rooms, surrounded by books, empty wine bottles, and overflowing ashtrays. However, toward the end of his stay he underwent a profound change in conduct and appearance, followed then by a period of extreme depression. Shortly thereafter he departed without farewells, leaving behind nothing but a manuscript which the young man now chooses to publish as "a document of the times" (205),[2] for in retrospect he discerns that the affliction which disturbed Haller was symptomatic of the times, and not simply the malady of an individual.

Yet more important than this external information is the view of Haller which we receive through the eyes of a young member of the bourgeoisie before we ever meet him in his own manuscript. The editor, by his own admission, is "a bourgeois, orderly person, used to work and the exact disposition of time" (196); he drinks nothing stronger than mineral water and abhors tobacco; he feels uncomfortable in the presence of illness, whether physical or mental; and he is inclined to be suspicious of anything which does not correspond to the facts of ordinary existence as he knows it. Haller offends all of these sensibilities and many others. He makes it clear that Haller was by no means a man congenial to his own temperament: "I feel myself deeply disturbed and disquieted by him, by the very existence of such a being, though I have actually become quite fond of him (189–190).

Yet despite his bourgeois inhibitions the young man is portrayed as an intelligent and reliable observer. His affection and interest allow him to perceive the conflict which disturbs Haller:

> In this period I became more and more aware that the illness from which he suffered arose not from any faults in his nature, but rather from the richness of his gifts and powers, which had not achieved harmony. (193)

He reveals for the first time in the course of the book the arbitrary dichotomy into Steppenwolf and Bürger, by which Haller chooses to designate the two polar aspects of his personality. The introduction, then, states the two conflicting themes and, without full comprehension of their meaning, portrays Haller in both capacities. The young man narrates the facts of Haller's life without ascribing to them the import which they assume in Haller's own mind.

The opening pages of the manuscript itself recount one typical evening in the life of the 48-year-old *littérateur* Harry Haller. In atrabilious words he portrays his state of mind, his beliefs and goals, his erratic existence up to the present date. His remarks actually parallel the comments of the introduction, and in many cases the specific events mentioned are identical in both sections. But Haller's remarks are on a different plane: whereas the introduction depicted him externally from

[2]*All page references to* Steppenwolf *are taken from Vol. IV of Hesse's* Gesammelte Dichtungen *([Frankfurt am Main]: Suhrkamp Verlag, 1952)—hereafter cited as* GD.

the bourgeois standpoint, we now meet him psychologically as he elects to think of himself, and we feel the full effect of his ambivalent attitude toward the bourgeoisie. He acknowledges that he is out of place in normal society, and he leads the life of a lone wolf, always on the fringe of humanity. Yet he is beset by a continual yearning for all that has been left behind:

> I don't know why it is so, but I—the homeless Steppenwolf and lonely hater of the petty bourgeois world—I always live in proper bourgeois houses; that's an old sentimental foible of mine. I dwell neither in palaces nor in the houses of the proletariat, but always precisely in these highly respectable, highly boring, scrupulously maintained petty bourgeois nests . . . . I love this atmosphere no doubt from my childhood, and my secret longing for something like a home leads me again and again, hopelessly, along these stupid old paths. (210)

The conflict is elucidated with many pertinent examples as Haller contemplates his existence and its value in the course of an evening walk.

These speculations are interrupted by the interpolation of the "Tract," a document which Haller acquires on this walk and takes home to read. Since the "Tract" is of central importance in the novel, it is necessary to recall briefly how it comes into Haller's hands. Wandering down a familiar alley that evening, he perceives a previously unnoticed doorway in the wall. Above the door is affixed a placard on which he is able to make out the fleeting, almost illegible words:

Magic Theater
Admission not for everyone
—not for everyone (215)

As he steps closer, the evanescent words vanish, but he glimpses a few letters which seem to dance across the wet pavement: "For madmen only!" After a time Haller proceeds to his restaurant, still musing over the significance of the queer letters he had seen or imagined. Out of curiosity, he passes back through the same alley later in the night and notes that the door and sign are no longer there. Suddenly a man emerges from a side street, trudging wearily and bearing a placard. Haller calls to him and asks to be shown the sign. Again he discerns "dancing, tumbling letters" (222):

Anarchistic Evening Entertainment
Magic Theater
Admission not for ev. . . (223)

But when he greets the bearer and seeks further information, the man mutters indifferently, hands him a small pamphlet, and disappears into a doorway. Upon his return home Haller sees that the pamphlet is entitled "The Tract of the Steppenwolf." At this point its text follows.

This "Tract," as Haller reads to his astonishment, offers still a third description of Harry Haller, the Steppenwolf. Whereas the first represented the objective but superficial impressions of a typical Bürger, and the second the subjective interpretation of the subject himself, this third depiction is the observation of a higher intelligence which is able to view Haller perspectively *sub specie aeternitatis*.

The "Tract," in essence, makes a distinction between three types of beings, differentiated relatively according to their degree of individuation. The remarkable cosmology which is developed here can best be visualized by the analogy of a sphere situated on an axis whose poles represent the opposite concepts of nature and spirit. The center of the sphere, as the point farthest removed from all extremes, is the bourgeois ego; the cosmic regions outside the sphere, on the other hand, are inhabited by the "tragic natures" or "Immortals" who have transcended the narrow bourgeois concept of egoism and have burst forth into the cosmos by embracing a belief in the fundamental unity of life. They are aware of the fact that supreme existence consists in the recognition and acceptance of all aspects of life, and this attitude demands transcendence of the ego in the bourgeois sense. In order to preserve his "Ich," his ego, the Bürger must resist every impulse to lose himself in extremes: he must sway toward neither pole; he wishes to be neither profligate nor saint. Moreover, in maintaining this position of moderation, the Bürger assumes a definite standpoint with regard to the world, relative to which certain of its polar opposites must be condemned as evil.

Thus, for the Bürger, whose very way of life requires the utmost order in the world, the opposite extreme of disorder or chaos must be anathema. The Immortals, on the contrary, accept chaos as the natural state of existence, for they inhabit a realm where all polarity has ceased and where every manifestation of life is approved as necessary and good. In their eyes the polarity of nature and spirit does not exist, for their cosmos is expansive enough to encompass all of the apparent polar extremes in the Bürger's limited sphere.

If the Immortals and the Bürger represent the two extremes in Hesse's scale of individuation, the Steppenwolf occupies a tenuous and anomalous perch between them:

> If we examine in this light the soul of the Steppenwolf, then he appears as a person who is destined alone by his high degree of individuation to be a nonbourgeois. For all highly developed individuation turns against the ego and tends towards its destruction. (238)

Yet not every person of this nature is strong enough to transcend the *principium individuationis* completely: many are destined to remain in the world of the Bürger despite their longing for the reaches of the cosmos. If we adapt this fact to the sphere image, we must place the Steppenwolf in an orbit within the sphere, cruising close to the surface, but never penetrating into the cosmos for more than a brief, tantalizing moment. The fact that he belongs to neither realm completely accounts for the Steppenwolf's dissatisfaction with existence and demonstrates why Harry Haller, the case in point, can find no satisfactory solution to his dilemma and often contemplates suicide.

The "Tract" goes on to point out that only humor can make it possible for the Steppenwolf to exist peacefully in a world whose values he despises:

> To live in the world as if it were not the world, to obey the law and yet to stand above the law, to possess, "as if one did not possess," to sacrifice as if it were no sacrifice—all these beloved and often formulated claims of a higher wisdom only humor is capable of realizing. (240)

But humor in this sense is possible only if the individual has resolved the conflicts in his own soul, and this resolution is the result of self-recognition. To this end the "Tract" mentions three contingencies for Haller:

> It is possible that he will one day come to know himself—by getting hold of one of our little mirrors, or by meeting the immortals, or perhaps by finding in one of our magic theaters what he needs to free his depraved soul. (241)

Thus the "Tract" proposes a reconciliation of the conflicting themes which have been discussed. If Harry Haller can peer deep into the chaos of his own soul by any of the suggested means, then he will be able to live happily in the world or even dare to make "the leap into the universe" (240)—to join the Immortals. The final section of the "Tract" explains, however, that this is a more difficult task than Harry had previously imagined, for his personality comprises not only the two conflicting poles which he had named, but literally thousands of divergent aspects which cry for recognition.

It becomes clear that the "Tract" is ostensibly the work of the Immortals, for no one else could have this lofty and all-encompassing view of the world. Thus it represents a study of Haller from still a third standpoint. If we pause now to survey the preliminary material of the novel, a pattern seems to emerge. These three sections (introduction, the opening pages of the manuscript, and "Tract") present three treatments of the conflicting themes in Haller's soul, as perceived respectively from the three points of view outlined in the theoretical tract: Bürger—Steppenwolf—Immortals. The introduction states the two themes theoretically; the second section brings the development in which the significance of these themes for Haller's life is interpreted; and the "Tract" recapitulates the themes, theoretically again, and proposes a resolution of the conflict. But this scheme, exposition—development—recapitulation, can be found in any book of music theory under the heading "sonata form" or "first-movement form," for it is the classical structure for the opening section of the sonata.

The terms "sonata" and "sonata form" are two of the most confusing designations in music theory, for the latter does not refer to the form of the former. The sonata is a generic name for any major composition of one to four movements, of which one (usually the first) must be in "sonata form." If the composition is written for piano, it is a piano sonata; if written for the orchestra, it is called a symphony; and so forth. The term which interests us here, "sonata form," refers to the structure of the first movement alone. The exposition states two themes with one in the tonic, the other in the dominant; the development follows in which the potentialities of these themes are worked out; and the recapitulation restates the themes as they occurred in the exposition, but this time both are in the tonic; the conflict has been resolved.

In the novel the difference in keys is approximated by the contrasting attitudes of Harry Haller as Steppenwolf, on the one hand, and as Bürger, on the other: the first represents, as it were, the tonic, and the second the dominant. The ABA structure of the sonata, which is achieved through the general repetition of the exposition in the recapitulation, is imitated by Hesse insofar as the exposition and recapitulation are views of Haller from the outside and are largely theoretical; this gives them the effect of unity. The development, however, differs from these in tone and style since it is written by Haller himself, and it stresses the practical significance of the two themes for his own life. The resolution of the tonic and dominant in the recapitulation is an obvious parallel to the proposed reconciliation of Steppenwolf and Bürger in Harry Haller. In view of this rather close correspondence between the musical form and the first part of *Steppenwolf,* it seems safe to assert that the preliminary material of the novel reveals "first-movement form." And in view of Hesse's chosen analogy, it would not be unreasonable to assume that this structure is a conscious one.

In case this assertion seems to force one art form willfully into the Procrustean bed of another, it might be mentioned in passing that "first-movement form" has been applied to various literary genres before now. Otto Ludwig, in his essay on "The General Form of Shakespearean

Composition,'' evolves a general structural tendency in Shakespeare's plays which he compares to sonata form. Oskar Walzel, ever the advocate of ''reciprocal illumination of the arts,'' suggests that the same application can be made to certain poems. H. A. Bosilius has shown that Thomas Mann's *Tonio Kröger* is consciously constructed according to the pattern of sonata form; and Calvin S. Brown, in *Music and Literature: A Comparison of the Arts,* devotes an entire chapter to the analysis of literary works—mainly poems—which employ this structure more or less successfully.[3]

On the other hand, there have been objections to the application of musical form to literary works, and one of the most lucid and convincing of these is stated in *Theory of Literature*, by René Wellek and Austin Warren (New York, 1949). With regard to romantic notions concerning musical form, the authors contend that ''blurred outlines, vagueness of meaning, and illogicality are not, in a literal sense, 'musical' at all'' (126). But we have seen that Hesse presents his material clearly, is specific in meaning, and proceeds according to a highly logical system. Wellek and Warren go on to say:

> Literary imitations of musical structures like leitmotif, the sonata, or symphonic form seem to be more concrete; but it is hard to see why repetitive motifs or a certain contrasting and balancing of moods, though by avowed intention imitative of musical composition, are not essentially the familiar literary devices of recurrence, contrast and the like which are common to all the arts. (126)

Yet Hesse, though he makes ample use of the leitmotif, depends neither upon this nor upon contrast in order to produce his musical effect; he is not concerned with vague synesthesia. Rather, he has devised a novel which consciously adheres to the rigid structure of ''sonata form,'' and the other musical devices which he employs are merely embellishments within the entire framework. Thus the criticism, which is justifiable with regard to many so-called musical works of literature, is not applicable in the case of *Steppenwolf*.

II

Before going on to the second part, we must pause to consider a matter which contains the key to the entire work: the question of double perception.

[3]Calvin S. Brown, ''Sonata Form,'' *Music and Literature: A Comparison of the Arts* (Athens, Georgia, 1948), pp. 161–177. This is unquestionably the most comprehensive and most perceptive book on the subject; it is regrettable that it does not include a historical survey of critical theory regarding the relationship of the two arts.

In the "Tract" we read: "And all this is known to the Steppenwolf, even if he never gets to see this sketch of his inner biography. He senses his position in the universe, he senses and knows the immortals" (241). This seems to suggest a satisfactory solution to the mystery of the "Tract." The device of causing a figure in a novel to read his own biography, written by some unknown hand, is an approved romantic practice, and Hesse is certainly an heir of romanticism. Yet it must not be forgotten that up to this point the entire work has taken place on the level of everyday reality. Why should there be this sudden intrusion of the supernatural? Is it not more reasonable to assume that Haller himself reads this strange message into the text of the pamphlet since it is all familiar to him? This is an intriguing speculation, but it requires substantiation.

In his essay "On Reading Books" (1920) Hesse considers three types of readers. The first type is the naïve person who accepts the book and its story objectively; the second type comprises those who read with the imagination of a child and comprehend the hundreds of symbolic connotations latent in every word and image. But the third reader is one who uses the book simply as a *terminus a quo:* on this level

> we no longer read at all what is on the paper before us, but rather we swim in the stream of suggestions and ideas that come to us from what we have read. They may come from the text, they may even come from the printed image. An ad in the newspaper can become a revelation.[4]

This delightful conceit is not the whim of an instant; it is a recurrent theme in Hesse's works. An example can be found, for instance, as much as ten years later in *Narcissus and Goldmund* (1930). After his rude awakening by Narcissus, Goldmund lives in a new world:

> A Latin initial became the perfumed face of his mother, a drawn-out tone in the Ave became the Gate of Paradise, a Greek letter became a running horse, a rearing snake. Quietly it coiled away among the flowers, and already in its place, there stood again the stiff page of the grammer book.[5]

In the light of this idea, why should the action in *Steppenwolf* not be construed similarly? Let us briefly reconstruct the scene. In a fit of depression Haller goes out for his evening stroll; he is willing to grasp eagerly after any ray of hope which would alleviate his desperate condition. Thus, when he notices a smudge or crack in the wall of the alley, set

---

[4]*Betrachtungen* (Berlin, 1928), p. 164; or *GS*, VII, 245.
[5]*GD*, V, 67.

off by the sparkle of the damp plaster, his overwrought mind reads an imaginary message in fleeting letters. In the course of the evening he consumes a considerable portion of wine: "I needed no more wine. The golden trace had sparked, I was reminded of eternity, of Mozart, of the stars" (219). In this inebriated and rhapsodic state he meets a weary placard-bearer, fortuitously, in the same fateful alley. But the tired worker, anxious to get rid of the troublesome drunk, brusquely shoves a pamphlet into his hands—*any* pamphlet— which Haller's acrobatic and stimulated mind converts, at home, into the "tract." These are essential thoughts from a remote and more perceptive area of Haller's intelligence—an area which is usually blocked by the problematics of his dual personality and the exigencies of his existence. Here, for an instant, his higher acumen seeps through.

This concept of double perception plays an increasingly important role in the novel, for it is necessary throughout the remainder of the book to make a clear distinction between two levels of reality: the everyday plane of the Bürger or the placard-bearer and the exalted, supernal plane of the Immortals and the magic theater. Haller might be called an eidetic, i.e., "an individual capable of producing subjective (visual or other) images or 'Anschauungsbilder' of virtually hallucinatory vividness." Accordingly, his experiences on the upper level of reality assume fully as much intensity for him as the action on the level of mundane reality.

Here again we are concerned with a highly musical device corresponding closely to counterpoint, which the *Harvard Dictionary of Music* defines as "the combination into a single musical fabric of lines or parts which have distinctive melodic significance."[6] By means of double perception almost any given action of the book may be interpreted on two distinct levels, and this produces the effect of simultaneity or concomitance of the two planes or melodic lines. This particular device comes much closer to the musical concept of *Point Counter Point* than the technique employed, for instance, by Aldous Huxley in his novel of that title or by André Gide or by many of their imitators. The latter achieve their effect by the sudden juxtaposition of various moods and points of view, but Hesse consciously attempts to produce authentic counterpoint by bringing the two lines of action into play at the same time.

In his chapter on "Timbre, Harmony, and Counterpoint," Calvin S. Brown denies the possibility of true counterpoint in literature, but he cites the literary pun as the closest approach. The limiting element in the case of the pun is the fact that we have "not two things, but one word with different relationships."[7] On the basis of this parallel it might be stated

---

[6] Willi Apel, *Harvard Dictionary of Music* (Cambridge, Mass., 1955), p. 189.
[7] *Music and Literature*, p. 42.

that double perception achieves the effect of a sustained pun, and the interplay of the two levels of reality produces a genuine contrapuntal effect. If this is not precisely what is understood by the musical concept of counterpoint, it at least represents an advance beyond any previous literary counterpart.

III

The second and longest part of *Steppenwolf* might be called Harry Haller's *Apprenticeship*, and it is interesting to note that the verbs *lernen* (to learn) and *lehren* (to teach) actually occur scores of times in this section of the book. Here Haller learns to accept many facets of life which certain inhibitions of his personality had previously caused him to reject; he discovers to his astonishment that the poles of his being are not so irreconcilable as he had imagined. This phase of Haller's education is rather elementary: it is kept on the level of everyday life in preparation for and in conscious anticipation of the more metaphysical scope of the magic theater.

The motif of "chance" and "destiny," as in *Wilhelm Meister's Apprenticeship*, lends an aura of inevitability to the initial events of the denouement, and it is an obvious corollary to the technique of double perception. One day Haller happens to see a man who resembles the placard-bearer of his recent adventure. With a conspiratorial wink Haller asks him if there is no entertainment that evening: " 'Evening Entertainment,' mumbled the man and looked at me blankly. 'Go to the *Schwarzer Adler*, fella, if you need something like that!' " (206). The repeated use of the word "seemed" in connection with these incidents indicates clearly that Haller is not dealing with the same man as before. Moreover, it is just chance that the stolid citizen happens to respond indignantly to the misunderstood question and advises Haller to go to an obviously notorious prostitute den if he wishes to satisfy his needs. It is likewise chance (or destiny?) which leads Haller that very evening to this particular nightclub, where he meets Hermine, who becomes his teacher during this *Apprenticeship*.

The entire first day of the action represents an accumulation of impossible situations which bring Haller to the point of suicide. One incident after another convinces him that his life has become intolerable. The conflict of themes which was introduced in the preliminary material is elevated in the course of this first day to an unbearable pitch. Late in the night Haller weaves wearily from bar to bar, determined to put an end to his miserable existence, yet hesitant to go home and do so. Then he finds himself outside the bar ''Zum schwarzen Adler,'' and since he recalls the name from that morning, he goes in.

It is made sufficiently clear in the course of the book that Hermine is a high-class prostitute or call girl, and she greets the errant Haller with an intimate, hearty tone which has no deep metaphysical implications whatsoever (as some scholars assume), but which is simply customary in her profession. She immediately perceives that he is weary, dejected, and drunk; like any sensible woman she advises him to sleep it off. Haller, drunk as he is and happy to be able to stave off his suicide as long as possible, is delighted to obey her. He feels that her immediate comprehension of his situation is almost preternatural. Actually, any reader will recognize that most of Hermine's remarks, like the utterances of the Delphic oracle, are open to two interpretations. In this case Hermine's words are precisely what one would expect from a prostitute with long experience in handling drunks and mothering would-be suicides. Only Haller's lonely and despondent state allows him to ascribe any higher significance to her casual remarks.

Hermine, who becomes genuinely interested in Haller, makes a tremendous impression on the naïve intellectual. In his eyes she stands for a wholly new aspect of life—one which he had previously regarded with distrust. His experiences with her must be viewed continually in double perspective. On the one hand, the whole episode is anticipated in the ''Tract,'' which, as an example of Haller's dual nature and bourgeois limitations, cites his attitude toward prostitutes:

> Besides, he had received a petty-bourgeois upbringing and had retained a number of concepts and models. Theoretically he hadn't the slightest objection to prostitution, but would be incapable of personally taking a prostitute seriously or of considering her his equal. (235–36)

Yet in order to overcome these bourgeois inhibitions he must expand his soul to the point of embracing every aspect of life (250). Hermine, then, is a test case: on a higher level Haller's acceptance of her and her world—dancing and jazz, the love orgies of Pablo and Maria, narcotics and the elemental pleasures of life—is only symbolic for his repudiation of the entire narrow world of the Bürger and his new dimensions as an aspirant to the kingdom of the Immortals.

Haller learns much from and through Hermine. She teaches him to enjoy and appreciate many new aspects of life, and her friends, Pablo and Maria, aid her in Haller's education. For Haller she becomes almost a symbol; he calls her ''a door through which life came to me!'' (290). On the brink of a suicide of despair he has found someone who can bring him back to life:

> She was salvation, the path to freedom. She had to teach me to live or to die. With her firm and pretty hand she had to touch my frozen heart and make it blossom from the touch of life or fall to ashes. (294)

Hermine, too, realizes why he needs her: "You need me to learn how to dance, to laugh, to live" (300). And at first she feels that the task is almost insurmountable: "I believe you must learn everything that others take for granted, even the pleasure of eating" (301). It is the art of life in which Hermine is Haller's preceptress:

> It is up to me to see that you learn the small, easy arts and games of life. In this area I am your teacher and I will be a better teacher for you than your ideal beloved was, you can be sure! . . . My friend, you undoubtedly excel at loving ideally and tragically. I don't doubt it. Congratulations! Now you will learn to love in a more common and more human way. (318)

But all that Haller learns from Hermine on this level of mundane reality is only symbolic for an entire new world of experiences: "Just as the gramophone ruined the air of ascetic intellectuality in my study . . . new, feared and disrupting things pressed from all sides into my so sharply defined and strictly isolated life" (319).

Yet on a higher level of reality Hermine and Pablo, the jazz musician to whom she introduces Haller, are equally important: as reflections of his own thoughts! For occasionally these two representatives of the sensual world utter deep and significant statements which ill conform to the very realistic picture drawn of them. Hermine, for example, expresses quite lucidly the central tenet of the novel, which Haller is unable to formulate articulately for himself; she confirms his inchoate belief in the eternal spiritual kingdom of the Immortals. She tells him what people of their sort, the Steppenwolf-natures, live for:

> It is not fame. Oh, no! But what I call eternity. The pious call it the kingdom of God. I think that we humans, we who are more demanding, we who have a longing, who have an extra dimension—we could not live if there were not a different air to breathe besides the air of this world, if there were not eternity as well as time, and that is the kingdom of the genuine. (345)

Just as Haller read his own speculations on the Steppenwolf into an indifferent pamphlet, so has he transplanted his own thoughts into the words of a clever courtesan. This fact is stressed: "It seemed to me that these were perhaps not her thoughts, but my own, which the clairvoyant girl had read and breathed in and returned to me, so that they now had form and stood as though new before me" (346). It is again made explicit at the end (411).

In the case of Pablo, who is presented consistently as a monosyllabic sensualist, it is even more striking. At the beginning of the magic theater, when Pablo is speaking so astutely on the nature of the personality, Haller muses:

> Was it not I, perhaps, who made him speak, who spoke through him? Was it not my own soul that looked at me from his black eyes . . . as from Hermine's grey eyes? . . . He, whom I had never heard speak coherently, who was interested in no dispute, no formulation, to whom I had not attributed the ability to think, he spoke now, he spoke with his good, warm voice fluently and without error. (367–368)

Thus, Hermine, Pablo, Maria, and the entire demimonde of *Steppenwolf* exist on a realistic plane consistently throughout the book. Only Haller's sense of double perception bestows upon them the added dimension by which they assume symbolic proportions. In the "Tract" he tells himself that he must expand his soul to encompass the world: accident with an element of destiny places him in a position to carry out this self-admonishment, and he sparks his contact with this other world with reflections which he imputes to the minds of his new acquaintances. This entire sequence of development, on both levels of reality, culminates in the experience of the magic theater, which takes place a little less than four weeks after the initial encounter with Hermine.

The occasion which Haller designates as the "magic theater" on the upper level of reality is no more than the aftermath of a great ball—according to the season probably a *Faschingsball*. Haller is prepared for it on both levels: he has learned to dance and to love; by implication he has embraced and affirmed all aspects of life. Symbolic for this acceptance of the cosmos, including its most abysmal depths, is the fact that Haller must descend to a basement bar, called quite pointedly "Hell," in order to meet Hermine (357). From that point they gradually ascend to a small room in the upper stories (367) where Haller later experiences the magic theater. This upward progression is interrupted by a symbolic wedding dance which Haller performs with Hermine (365) and which represents the imminent marriage of the two poles of existence in his soul: the intellectual or spiritual with the sensual or natural. In this passage Hermine is no longer "*a* woman"; she is "womankind": "All women of this feverish night . . . melted together into a single one, who blossomed in my arms" (365).

In the course of the symbolic ascent, on both planes, Haller loses the last vestiges of his bourgeois notion of individuality. Here the concept of fluidity, so important in other works by Hesse (e.g., *Siddhartha*), is touched upon: "I was no longer myself. My personality was dissolved in the carnival frenzy like salt in water'' (362). These rites are the final stage in Haller's initiation for the supreme experience. Only now can he agree to Pablo's invitation to the magic theater, which involves the stipulation: ''Admission for madmen only—you pay with your reason'' (367).

The words ''only for madmen,'' which occur in leitmotif fashion at several significant points in the book, sum up still another major motif of the novel: namely, the concept of magical thinking. This idea is most succinctly stated in the essay ''Thoughts on Dostoevsky's *Idiot*'' (1919)[8], in which Hesse declares that the ''madmen'' are those rare individuals, like Myschkin in Dostoevski's novel, who have perceived the total relativity of good and evil; they are the inhabitants of this world who have learned to regard life with the eyes of the Immortals. They live for a higher reality where polar opposites have ceased to be reciprocally hostile, where every aspect of life is affirmed, where there is no dichotomy between *fas* and *nefas*. They think ''magically,'' for they look beyond the apparent ''reality'' of the bourgeois phenomenal world to the essential reality of cosmic harmony.

After his symbolic descent into hell and the wedding dance with his opposite and complement, Hermine, Haller is able to think magically and to accept Pablo's invitation, even on the condition that he become ''mad.'' This acceptance concludes Haller's *Apprenticeship*: the second part of the novel has portrayed the full course of his development from a schizophrenic intellectual contemplating suicide because of an imaginary conflict between two poles of his being, to a man with a healthy awareness and appreciation of the world around him. To extend the analogy, he is now ready to embark on his *Journeyman's Travels*, to plumb the very depths of the potentialities of his life. The magic theater is the vehicle through which he is to be introduced symbolically to the full extent of his personality in all its manifestations, and the consummation of his symbolic marriage to Hermine is to represent the complete welding of all aspects of his nature.

It would be gratifying if we could demonstrate that this second part conforms strictly to the form of the second movement of the sonata, but that would be an extension of the truth. The second movement offers various possibilities to the composer, but since no precise correspondence exists between the novel and the musical forms, it will be best not to go into the matter. It might be mentioned in passing that the structure of many modern sonatas is far less rigid than that of the classical sonata, and we have seen that Haller's *Apprenticeship* is highly musical in nature owing to the device of double perception or counterpoint. In this restricted sense, then, the second part is equivalent to a second movement.

[8]*GS*, VII, especially pp. 181–184.

IV

The "magic theater," like every other incident in the novel, is open to interpretation on two levels. On the realistic level it is nothing more than an opium fantasy in which Haller indulges after the ball in the company of Hermine and Pablo. From the very beginning of Haller's acquaintance with Pablo it is emphasized that the jazz musician is familiar with all the exotic refinements of narcotics. At their first meeting Pablo offers Haller a powder to improve his spirits:

> In fact I soon became fresher and more cheerful. Probably some cocaine was in the powder. Hermine told me that Pablo had such drugs, that he acquired them from secret sources, that he served them up occasionally to his friends, and that he was a master at mixing and determining their dosages: drugs . . . to bring forth beautiful dreams. (322)

Later Haller admits: "I often partook of his drugs" (336). On the last evening Pablo again offers Haller one of his stimulants:

> Each of us smoked now . . . slowly on his cigarette, whose smoke was as thick as incense, and drank in slow swallows the bittersweet . . .liquid that was actually invigorating and cheering, as if one were being filled with gas and losing one's weight. (368)

Everything Haller is to see in the magic theater, then, is a reflection of his own soul and a product of his eidetic vision under the influence of narcotics. Pablo makes this clear:

> You know where this other world lies hidden, that it is the world of your own soul that you seek. Only within yourself does that other reality that you long for dwell. I can give you nothing that does not exist within yourself. . . . I help to make your own world visible to you. That is all. (368–69)

The "Tract of the Steppenwolf," as we recall, stated that the Immortals are those who have transcended the *principium individuationis*. Pablo now restates this theme:

> Without doubt you have already guessed that the conquest of time, escape from reality, or whatever you want to call your longing, is nothing more than the wish to be freed from your so-called personality. (370)

The magic theater gives Haller a chance to do precisely this. Peering into Pablo's magic mirror, Haller perceives simultaneously thousands of faces of his personality: he sees himself as a child, a youth, an adult, an old man; as a serious scholar and a comical buffoon; bald and with long hair; every potentiality of development and expression is there in the mirrored image.[9] When he accepts the fact that all of these Harrys are part of his own personality, he is prepared to enter the magic theater and to enjoy the multifarious activities offered there for his amusement.

Structurally the theater which he visualizes in this dream is on the order of a penny arcade. There are thousands of booths which he has only to enter in order to undergo a new experience. Hesse mentions fifteen of these sideshows by name, and Haller enters only four of them. But it is obvious that these few sensations are symbolic for the world of experience which lies open to him.

Individually each sideshow recapitulates a motif which has been developed in the course of the entire novel, and each one can be analyzed separately in order to demonstrate how carefully Hesse has constructed his work. Let us examine the first one as a typical example. While Haller is peering into Pablo's magic mirror, two aspects of the personality which he sees reflected there leap out of the mirror: one, an elegant young man, embraces Pablo and goes off with him; the other, a charming youth of sixteen or seventeen, dashes down the corridor to a booth marked "All girls are yours!" (373). In the second part of the novel it is indicated that Pablo, apart from his proficiency in heterosexual love, is also homosexually inclined; on two specific occasions he makes overtures to Haller, who rejects them indignantly. Now Haller sees that part of his personality is not only willing but eager to explore this particular side of life. Yet at the same time another part of his nature goes into a booth where (as we learn later when Haller finally comes back to the same booth himself) he experiences the love of every woman Haller has ever known or even seen and desired during his life. The complete resolution of any polarity in matters of physical love is clearly implied.

The following sideshows pick up various other motifs from the novel: in the second one Haller learns that he, the confirmed pacifist, is able to enjoy war and killing. The motifs of metamorphosis, suicide, the decline of Western Civilization, the nature of music, humor, the structure of the personality—all these are mentioned, and each one, whether Haller actually enters the booth or not, conjures up a very concrete image because it represents the culmination of a motif which has been subtly suggested again and again throughout the book.[10]

[9]This effect, which has much in common with the painting "I and the Village" by Chagall, is a favorite motif in Hesse's works and may be found also in *Klingsor's Last Summer* (1919), *GD*, III, 611–112, as well as in *Siddhartha* (1922), *GD*, III 731–732.

[10]It is almost superfluous to mention that all of these motifs play a major role in most of Hesse's other works and do not belong exclusively to *Steppenwolf*.

The final tableau, however, requires a more detailed consideration, for there the two levels of reality become so entangled as to be almost inextricable. As the effect of the opium begins to wear off, Harry has his most sublime experience: direct contact with the Immortals in the person of Mozart (like an earlier encounter with Goethe in a dream). But this exposure is too much for his overtaxed nerves: he feels despondent of ever attaining the stature of the Immortals, whom, for an instant, he felt that he had approximated. In this feeling of despair he suddenly becomes aware that Pablo and Hermine, far from spending their time in idle dreams, are lying on the carpet, locked in a passionate embrace. On the dream level Haller seems to take a knife and kill Hermine (406). Yet the actual event probably amounts to no more than an exclamation of jealousy and disgust when he realizes that the woman whom he had elevated to symbolic stature, rather than being the ethereal personification of an ideal, is indeed very much of the flesh. It is, to be sure, a murder on this level of reality also, for in his mind he eradicates the idealized image of Hermine which had obsessed him. As he contemplates her (imagined) corpse, he meditates: "Now her wish was fulfilled. Before she had become completely mine, I had killed my beloved" (406).

This realization marks the climax of the novel, for the whole structure is calculated to bring Haller to the consummation of his wedding with Hermine, to the total acceptance of all that she represents to him: namely, the opposite of every pole of his personality. He fails because he allows a touch of bourgeois reality to creep into the images of the magic theater; he allows bourgeois jealousy to destroy the image of Hermine as the complement of his being. Pablo's words indicate that Hermine, in the last analysis, is simply an aspect of Haller's being with which he is not yet reconciled: "You did not know how to manage with this figure—I believed you had learned the game better than that. Well, it can be remedied" (414).

After the deed Haller slumps back in his chair, and when Pablo fetches a blanket to cover Hermine from the cool morning air (on the level of ordinary reality), he interprets it to be a cover to conceal the knife wound (on the dream level.) When Pablo brings in a radio (first level), Haller thinks that it is Mozart again (second level), and the ensuing conversation is once more on the plane of dream or higher reality. Mozart-Pablo's message is a reiteration of the thought which Haller had once before inferred from Hermine's words. Mozart experiments with the radio and, at length, locates a Munich broadcast, where the strains of a Handel concerto are scarcely recognizable through the maddening static and interference of the instrument. When Haller objects to this, Mozart replies:

You are hearing and seeing, my dear friend, an excellent image of all life. When you listen to the radio you hear and see the primordial conflict between idea and appearance, between eternity and time, between the divine and the human. (409)

Haller must learn to perceive the eternal spirit behind the spurious phenomena of external reality; he must learn to take seriously only those things which deserve it: the essence, not the appearance. Mozart goes on to chastise Haller for the murder of the image of Hermine, and it is revealed that the stabbing took place only on the dream level. Before the jury of Immortals he accuses Haller: "Haller . . . insulted high art by confusing our lovely hall of images with so-called reality and by stabbing to death an imagined girl with an imagined knife" (412). For this crime against the higher reality of the Immortals Haller is punished by "being laughed at" (412).[11] The only penance imposed is the following:

You shall live, and you shall learn to laugh. You shall learn to listen to the accursed radio music of life, shall honor the spirit behind it, shall learn to laugh at the pother in it. That's all. No more is demanded of you. (413–414)

At this point Haller begins to realize that the figure which he had taken for Mozart is actually none other than Pablo, who is reproaching him for his previous outburst against Hermine. He comprehends that he was too weak to sustain the rarified stratosphere of the Immortals; he had confused the two levels of reality and had taken seriously the prostitute Hermine of the first level, whereas he should merely have laughed at her. By taking her seriously and allowing himself a tirade against her, he had destroyed the image of Hermine as the symbolic woman, which he had meticulously constructed during his four-week acquaintance with her.

However, the novel ends on an optimistic note, for Haller understands his situation and his shortcomings: "Some day I would play the game of figures better. Some day I would learn to laugh. Pablo would wait for me. Mozart would wait for me" (415). Haller knows now that Mozart and Pablo are only two aspects of the same person (just like Narcissus and Goldmund in Hesse's next novel): between the two of them they represent the complete union of the poles of spirit and nature. Haller's last words, with their tacit understanding and affirmation of this metaphysical union, indicate that he, too, may hope to learn magical thinking and to enter the ranks of the Immortals. He has experienced it briefly, but must transcend himself in order to be able to maintain constantly this new view of life.

[11]H. H. in Hesse's *Journey to the East* (1932) is punished more mildly for a similar transgression against the eternal spirit by being smiled at by the assembled Immortals; cf. *GD*, VI, 65. In the same book, moreover, Mozart appears disguised as Pablo; cf. *GD*, VI, 63.

Thus the novel ends. In retrospect the structure of the magic theater might be called a theme with variations. The theme, which is borrowed from the "Tract," is the notion that Haller's personality comprises a multiplicity of opposite elements; but when he views these opposites from the new perspective gained through the magic mirror, from the standpoint of the Immortals, he realizes that they are not mutually exclusive. For the duration of the magic theater—until the murder of Hermine's image—he observes life from a point outside the polar sphere of the Bürger, and he is able to accept all its aspects. Each booth in the magic theater represents a variation on this theme: in each one he sees a specific instance of the opposite tendencies in his nature, and yet he affirms all of them completely.

The *Harvard Dictionary of Music* defines the theme with variations as "a musical form based upon the principle of presenting a musical idea (theme) in an arbitrary number of modifications (from 4 to 30 or more), each of these being a 'variation' " (782). It also has a statement that the variation is sometimes employed as the form of the finale in the sonata or symphony (265). Calvin S. Brown mentions that the obvious danger of formal repetition and variation in the literary genres is tedium,[12] and in conventional works of literature that criticism holds true. By making use of a dream sequence Hesse is able to maintain a constant theme while providing in each case a different setting and new details. The setting and details, in turn, are drawn from motifs which occur in the preceding parts of the novel. Thus, the finale knits the book into a tightly constructed whole.

Steppenwolf might be compared to a sonata in three movements. The first movement shows unmistakable first-movement form, or the so-called sonata form; the second movement, though it does not reveal any form typical of the adagio of the sonata, employs the highly musical device of double perception or counterpoint throughout; the third movement, finally, is constructed according to a pattern remarkably similar to a finale in variations. As in the modern symphony, the themes are not limited to one movement alone, but appear in all the parts, thus creating an effect of structural unity in the whole: the second and third movements are based, respectively, upon the first and second points of the "Tract." Although the work abounds in so-called musical devices, like leitmotif and contrast, it does not depend upon such hazy concepts in order to attain its musical effect. Instead, it reveals a structure which, consciously or unconsciously on Hesse's part, corresponds in general to a specific musical form and, in certain places, seems to adhere rigidly to the accepted pattern of musical composition. To this extent it might be permissible to designate Hesse's *Steppenwolf* as a sonata in prose.

[12] *Music and Literature,* p. 111 and 134.

R. C. Andrews

The Poetry of Hermann Hesse

At a time when in much of Europe literature is in danger of being commandeered by political interests, and books turned into signposts to the right or left, it is pleasing to be able to salute the 75th birthday of Hermann Hesse, who has always stood *au-dessus de la mêlée*. To say that he is a descendant of the great eighteenth century, which he has called "the last great age of culture in Europe," is not to relegate him to the margin of modern life or to place him in some aesthetic cul-de-sac. For his nostalgia for a lost age is the humanist's nostalgia for a lost synthesis, and it carries with it a condemnation of our own age. As a disciple of Goethe Hesse has sought to attain the timeless wisdom of the master, the serenity which bridges over the chronic dualism of man. In offering as a birthday tribute this appreciation of his poems—in many ways the least representative but most personal part of his work—the writer would add the hope that Hermann Hesse, like his great predecessor in Weimar, will continue to enrich his world for many years after this, his 75th birthday.

The fundamental problematic underlying Hesse's poetry is the eternal conflict of the two souls. This at once spiritual, moral and aesthetic conflict is perhaps most clearly defined in his novel *Narcissus and Goldmund*, which provides a key to the less systematized philosophy of the poems. The novel traces the life story of two medieval figures, one belonging to the masculine world of the intellect, the other to the feminine world of the soul. The friendship between these two opposites bridges the gulf between them—the seemingly impassable gulf between intellect and instinct, reason and sensualism, morality and amorality, the scholar and the artist, the ascetic and the voluptuary, the masculine and the feminine. That both these figures attain to a final synthesis, that the artist is able to

Reprinted from German Life and Letters, *vol. 6 (1952) by permission of the publisher. English translations are by the editor.*

look upon his artistic creation as the involuntary giving of form to the Platonic "ideas" of the scholar, that the ascetic abbot, the student of Aristotle and St. Thomas Aquinas, with his strict intellectual discipline and logical thinking, is able finally to accept the dionysiac world of the senses as God-willed, is the fruit of their spiritual cross-pollination. It is natural that Hesse's deeper sympathies should lie throughout with Goldmund, the vagabond artist, whose life history is the striving of his feminine nature back to the primeval Mother and whose last words are a welcome to death, the return to the womb; for many of the poems are the confessions of another Goldmund, and only in the later poems is his own synthesis attained.

Hesse's collected poems, published in 1942,[1] run to over 400 pages. This considerable output is, by his own confession, the unsorted, unsifted and unpruned production of a lifetime. He defends his refusal to weed out obvious weaknesses: for him at least they have some meaning: "as a confession of what I have lived and done . . . as an acceptance of it all, including the faults and weaknesses. . . ." It would therefore be unfair to dwell upon the adolescent excesses of the early poems: the magical romanticism of moonlight, maidens on balconies, purple kisses, alcoves and crumbling ruins, and the Christmas-card prettiness of landscapes seen as though through a prism, of golden gondolas beneath blue Venetian skies. This refusal to conceal flaws in his poems is paralleled by a similar refusal to cloak the strident hedonism of his early manhood. The completeness of the poems matches the completeness of their testimony. They provide a moral photography of the poet's life—and if some of the prints are badly exposed, they are nevertheless part of the whole and have not been excluded.

The poems span the years from 1895 to 1941. They record the young poet's apprenticeship to life—the vagabondage of another Wayfaring Lad who took "wine, woman and song" as his creed, the unrepentant hedonism of another Shropshire Lad, but without his gestures of despair, the forever unrequited nostalgia of the sensualist, who longs for home when abroad, for love when alone, for the open road when sedentary, and whose gaze is continually turning back over his shoulder, lured by the mirage of the past. This instinctive acceptance of life is that of the poet "who drinks of life as other men drink wine." It is an aesthetic, non-materialistic sensualism which never hardens into ritual and whose most riotous orgies are savored with the deliberate perceptual refinement of the gourmet. With the passing of the years the tone of the poetry deepens, the clouds of two world wars darken them, modern civilization scrawls its question marks upon them, and Hesse the philosopher probes the ultimate

[1]Fretz & Wasmuth Verlag, Zürich.

meaning of life. Thus the poems record the moments of experience and the moments of wisdom of a lifetime, and the handwriting of an epoch is in them.

One of the earliest poems, "Geständnis" ("Confession"), begins thus:

> Wer meine Freunde sind?—
> Zugvögel, überm Ozean verirrt,
> Schiffbrüchige Schiffer, Herden ohne Hirt,
> Die Nacht, der Traum, der heimatlose Wind.

> (Who are my friends?—
> Migrating birds lost over the ocean,
> Shipwrecked seamen, herds without a shepherd,
> The night, the dream, the homeless wind.)

This picture of the lonely wayfarer, claiming kinship with the protean solitudes of nature, is one that recurs throughout the early poems, whose themes often recapture the romanticism of Eichendorff and Wilhelm Müller; for the young Hesse, a lone pilgrim far from home, communes with what is remote, ephemeral or unattainable in nature: with the stars, the sea, a drifting leaf, a wave, a boat adrift. A ship on the horizon, a fast flowing river, a flight of birds or the passage of clouds will awaken in him thoughts of home:

> Ich liebe die Weissen, Losen
> Wie Sonne, Meer und Wind,
> Weil sie der Heimatlosen
> Schwestern und Engel sind   ("Weisse Wolken")

> (I love the white ones, the loose ones,
> Sun, sea, wind,
> Because to the homeless
> They are sisters and angels.)   ("White Clouds")

The conflict in the wayfarer's heart between the call of home and the call of the horizon ripples the placidity of a number of poems, but only in later years does the poet discover why he prefers the horizon: only the wise know the art of living in peace in one place. Hesse prefers the zest and the torments of distance:

> Denn auch im Glücke kann ich auf Erden
> Doch nur ein Gast und niemals ein Bürger werden.
>   ("Gegenüber von Afrika")

> (For even in happiness I can, on Earth,
> Be only a guest and never a citizen.)   ("Across from Africa")

The early poems are content to record the courtship of the poet's senses and the beauties of nature, for the most part in fluent rhymed quatrains. The best of them ("Das Treibende Blatt," "Pilger," "Abends auf der Brücke,""Gang bei Nacht") ("The Falling Leaf," "Pilgrim," "Evening on the Bridge," "Walk at Night.") are characterized by a folk song simplicity which in the later poems takes on something of the reflective mantle of the "Spruch" ("Saying"). A hint of the later maturity sometimes breaks through the artless lyricism of the pilgrim's songs:

> Ein Sucher bin ich nur,
> Der durch die Welt in Sonne, Staub und Wind
> Begierig tastet nach der Schöpfung Spur.   ("Entschluss")

> (A seeker is what I am,
> Who, through the world in sun, dust and wind,
> Seeks hungrily the traces of creation.)   ("Decision")

At times the poet turns his gaze from the horizon to mourn at the grave of his childhood. Again and again the same sentiments recur: that there is no bridge leading back to the days that are gone, that the gay reality of the past has become a faded dream or that the red flame of youth has flickered out. Any sudden glimpse of natural beauty will bring the tears to his eyes: the red of the sunset, blossoms caught on the breeze, autumn mists, bells at eventide or the ring of children's songs. With their lyrical spontaneity and effortless technical mastery, these Chopinian impromptus on the loss of past joys are as it were belied by the smoothness of the verse, and at times the easy lilt of the rhythm does not conceal the tiredness and decadence to which the Neo-Romantics were prone.

The keenest memories of the past are those of past loves. Like Goldmund, the poet has roamed at random through the world and taken his pleasures where he found them. There are few true love poems here, but rather hymns to passion and laments over the sour aftertaste of satiety. "Juchhe! nun lodert alle Lust/Empor in gellen Flammen" ("Hurrah! Now passion flares,/flares up in shrill flames") is the characteristic cry of the adventurer at the sight of his latest conquest. The apotheosis of physical love and seduction finds its clearest expression in "Nelke" ("Carnation"): the flower has one impulse: "Rascher, heisser, wilder blühen!" ("To bloom more quickly, hotter, wilder!"); a flame in the breeze has one impulse: "Rascher, rauher zu verbrennen!" ("To burn up more quickly, more harshly!"); so love has one impulse too:

> Du in meinem Blute innen,
> Liebe du, was soll dein Träumen?
> Willst ja nicht in Tropfen rinnen,
> Willst in Strömen, willst in Fluten
> Dich vergeuden, dich verschäumen!
>
> (You who are within my blood,
> Dear you, why do you dream?
> You do not want to trickle in drops,
> You want to waste and foam yourself away
> In streams, in floods.)

This enthronement of the sensual, which leads the poet so easily from the contemplation of beautiful objects like a Stradivarius or a young birch to thoughts of his beloved, finds its natural sequel in the disillusion of fulfilled desire. Nowhere does this confession that lust is tinsel, not gold, achieve poetry; experience is not crystallized into image but rather loiters along in the declamatory privacies of the love letter. Only occasionally, when the sensual is forgotten (e.g., "Die Schöne," "Wenn doch mein Leben" ["Lovely One," "If Yet My Life"] is the restraint of the emotion reflected in the form. But rarely is "the dark river-god of the blood" forgotten, and it is hardly surprising that the last real love poem in the collection should end with the plea: "Mitten in den Flammen lass mich sterben!" ("Weg zur Mutter") ["In the midst of the flames let me die!" ("Way to the Mother")].

Throughout the poems the wayfarer's joys and sorrows have their setting in the landscapes of his travels—European, tropical and Oriental—and the small group of poems entitled *Gedichte des Malers* (*Poems of the Painter*) confirms the evidence of earlier poems that the poet can paint a landscape. "Augen, trinket die Farben in euch hinein!" ("Eyes, drink in the colors!") he cries in one of these poems—and it is not the only time he speaks in the accents of Keller. A plastic awareness of color and shape enables him to capture the essence of a scene or season in the confines of a single verse:

> Ein Wetterleuchten
> Beschaut sich bleich
> Mit grossen, feuchten
> Augen im Teich.   ("Frühsommernacht")

(A flash of lightning
Observes itself palely
With large, damp
Eyes, in the pond.)   ("Early Summer Night")

An dem grün beflognen Hang
Ist schon Veilchenblau erklungen,
Nur den schwarzen Wald entlang
Liegt noch Schnee in zackigen Zungen.   ("März")

(On the green-flown cliff
The blue of violets has already died away,
Only along the black woods,
Snow still lies in zigzag tongues.)   ("March")

Herbstregen hat im grauen Wald gewühlt,
Im Morgenwind aufschauert kalt das Tal,
Hart fallen Früchte vom Kastanienbaum
Und bersten auf und lachen feucht und braun.("Gang im Spätherbst")

(The autumn rain has rummaged in the woods,
In the morning wind the valley trembles with cold,
The fruits of the chestnut tree fall down hard
And burst open and laugh, damp and brown.)
                                        ("Walk in Late Autumn")

Not always does the rest of the poem fulfill the promise of the opening
lines, for the concluding sentiments, which are at times groping and
tentative, bring several of the poems to a lame ending. But the poet's
refusal to retouch his work makes such flaws inevitable. On the other
hand, where the landscape itself remains the main purpose of the poem
(e.g., "Windiger Tag im Juni," "Frühling in Locarno," "Dorfabend,"
"Heisser Mittag," "Augenblick vor dem Gewitter," "Alter Park"
["Windy Day in June," "Spring in Locarno," "Village Evening,"
"Hot Noon," "A Moment before the Storm," "Old Park"]), he often
achieves the impressionistic freshness and cavalier coloring of a Lilien-
cron. Implicit in all these poems is the poet's belief in the permanence of
natural beauty allied with the statement of man's impermanence. But
there always remains the eternal consolation of a return to the one and
ultimate Mother, a theme which finds its highest expression in the
philosophy of the later poems. For just as Goldmund, after a life apprenticeship to shape, color and touch, comes to look upon nature as his

Eternal Mother, so Hesse, consummating the marriage of sense and mind, progresses to a final pantheism:

> Gottes Atem hin und wider,
> Himmel oben, Himmel unten,
> Licht singt tausendfache Lieder,
> Gott wird Welt im farbig Bunten.   (''Magie der Farben'')

> (God's breath to and fro,
> Heaven above, heaven below,
> Light sings a thousand different songs,
> God becomes world in colorful variety.) (''The Magic of Colors'')

Thus nature becomes in turn scene, solace and sanctuary.

The elegiac sensuousness and undisciplined romanticism of these early poems leave memories of themes rather than of forms, for form with Hesse is derivative rather than original. They represent the poet's acceptance of a sensualism which goes beyond indulgence to affirmation. With the passing of the years, however, the poet turns his gaze more and more inward upon himself. A curtain of philosophy and mysticism is drawn across the unashamed Bacchanalianism of his early manhood; but the curtain is not a cloak—it veils but does not shut out the unreflecting gestures of the blood. Thus it is in the later poems that the problematic dualism of man, the tortured schizophrenia of the Steppenwolf, the conflict between Goldmund and Narcissus for the possession of his soul, is most marked and the quest for a synthesis more deliberate.

What may be called Hesse's philosophic poems—though the term itself is too suggestive of a doctrinal dogmatism which has no place in the poems—fall roughly into two groups: one deals with man's relationship to nature (i.e., to God), the second with the dualism of man's self.

The poet's attitude to nature passes from the spontaneous contact of the earlier poems to a deeper and conscious communion, which at its most intense becomes identification. The poet feels not only that his being is rooted in the same soil as tree, built of the same stone as mountain and pulsed with the same blood as bird—he actually feels himself tree, mountain and bird:

> In mir und ausser mir
> Ist ungeschieden, Welt und ich ist eins.
> Wolke weht durch mein Herz,
> Wald träumt meinen Traum,
> Haus und Birnbaum erzählt mir
> Die vergessene Sage gemeinsamer Kindheit . . .   (''Adagio'')

(What is in me and outside me
Is not separate, the world and I are one.
Clouds drift through my heart,
Woods dream my dream,
House and pear tree tell me
The forgotten saga of a common childhood.)   ("Adagio")

In the short poem "Spruch" ("Saying") this mystic pantheism rises from the intimacy of a prayer to the sanctity of a benediction:

So musst du allen Dingen
Bruder und Schwester sein,
Das sie dich ganz durchdringen
Dass du nicht scheidest Mein und Dein.

Kein Stern, kein Laub soll fallen—
Du musst mit ihm vergehn!
So wirst du auch mit allen
Allstündlich auferstehen.

(To all things must you
Brother and Sister be,
So that they permeate you so,
So that you not separate mine and yours.)

(No star, no leaves shall fall—
But you must die with them!
So will you then each hour
With all things rise again.)

But underlying this rhapsody is a more sombre tone, played on the cellos of lament. It is the consciousness of man's impermanence. "Uns ist kein Sein vergönnt" ("No existence is allowed us"), cries the poet in one of his finest poems, "Klage" ("Lament"). If only man could achieve the durability of stone—but no, he is swept away by the cosmic stream. Thus the earlier laments over lost youth and vanished love are here lifted onto a nobler plane; his nostalgia has gained a new dimension. But nowhere does lament degenerate into nihilistic despair, for the ultimate consolation of his pantheistic faith remains—the consolation that, whilst men depart, man remains. This pantheistic commonplace, already heightened into poetry in the second verse of "Spruch," is linked with Nietzsche's "eternal recurrence," whose formative influence is acknowledged, and has inspired some of the finest poems ("Manchmal," "Dorfkirchhof," "Unterwegs," "Wir leben hin . . . ," "Zusammenhang," "Neues Erleben") ("Sometimes," "Village Churchyard," "On the Way,"

"We live on . . . ," "Context," "New Experience"). In them man is portrayed as the heir of past eternities ("Ein Strahl bin ich des Lichts, ein Blatt am Baum/Unzähliger Geschlechter . . .") ("A beam I am of light, A leaf on the tree/Of untold generations . . .") and the ancestor of future eternities. Man stands at the conflux of two eternities, bearing the torch of life which was kindled by primeval fires, and with his eyes turned towards ever new suns.

Against the background of Hesse's Heraclitean view of life, death shrinks to human proportions. Indeed, when Hesse uses the terms "Mother Death" and "Brother Death," he is not just chanting the mystic's litany. "Mother" and "Brother" are here warm human concepts as much as the images of mystical longing. Death is just the final lone wayfarer whom the traveler meets on his journey through life. Why therefore stoicism or defiance? With his wineglass at his lips Hesse offers death his hand with an almost coquettish familiarity; elsewhere death is the kindly gardener, and even where he assumes the usual figure of the reaper, the emphasis is on the harvest and not on the sickle.

This idea of harvest, of ripeness and maturity, arises naturally from the poet's philosophy of "eternal recurrence." Death leads to rebirth—not in the Christian but in the seasonal sense. After the reds and golds of man's autumn he lies for a while like a seed beneath the snows or as a field lies fallow. Time and again the autumn scene inspires the poet to reflect on the rich mellowness of dying:

> Herbst, kühle mir das heisse Herz,
> Dass es gelinder schlage
> Und still durch goldene Tage
> Hinüberspiele winterwärts.   ("Oktober")

> (Autumn, cool my hot heart,
> That it beat mildly
> And quietly through golden days
> Play on towards winter.)   ("October")

This gentle gliding towards death with lilt of Rilke's swan is attained by those whose life has produced its harvest. Among the serenest poems are those pantheistic confessions of faith in which death is welcomed as a bridgehead between the individual life of a man and the cosmic life of the whole ("Erster Schnee," "Zeichen im Waldkeller," "Schnee") ("First Snow," "Signs in the Wood Cellar," "Snow"). This mysticism is forever seeking to crystallize itself in sensuous imagery; thus in "Ländlicher Friedhof" ("Country Churchyard") the poet links the dead in the graves below with the flowers and bees above: the former nourish the latter in the constant flux of death and rebirth; and in "Welkes Blatt" ("Dead Leaf") the poet bids the dead leaf not to resist the wind which seeks to snap its stalk of life and sweep it away. "Ripeness is all." These poems invariably take the form of a simple parallelism between an autumnal or wintry landscape in which nature, having passed through another life cycle, prepares serenely for another death, and man himself, whose death is but one of many deaths he is destined to die. Macrocosm and microcosm are one like the sea and the wave. Thus when the poet cries "Sterbenkönnen ist ein heiliges Wissen" ("Knowing how to die is holy knowledge"), we realize that this sacred wisdom is the acceptance of a pantheistic view of life, in which the indestructible soul of man is borne along by a protean life force and transmitted, a cosmic pulse beat, through grass, mountain, bird and beast, and onwards to man himself, in the bitter but triumphant path from death to birth. Nowhere has Hesse expressed this philosophy more poetically than in "Alle Tode" ("All Deaths"), whose opening lines have an almost Rilkean accent:

> Alle Tode bin ich schon gestorben,
> Alle Tode will ich wieder sterben,
> Sterben den hölzernen Tod im Baum,
> Sterben den steinernen Tod im Berg,
> Irdenen Tod im Sand,
> Blätternen Tod im knisternden Sommergras
> Und den armen blutigen Menschentod.

> (All deaths have I already died,
> All deaths will I die once again,
> Die the death of wood in the tree,
> Die the stone death in the mountain,
> Earthy death in the sand,
> Leaf death in the rustling summer grass.
> And the poor, bloody death of man.)

But the relative insignificance of one man's life does not release him from the perpetual civil war within himself. Each man's life is the plaything of two forces, mind and matter, and few there are who reach a synthesis. We turn therefore to the poets, the historians of this conflict, to see by what process they reached an armistice. Hesse, as we have seen from his novel *Narcissus and Goldmund*, posed the problem at its most acute by contrasting intellectual asceticism and renunciation of the flesh with a dionysiac affirmation of life, only to reach the conclusion that neither was a complete answer. But complete answers are rare and only reached after a lifetime of questioning. It is clear from the poems that

Hesse himself is another Goldmund, a creative artist whose senses are always alive to the shapes, sounds and colors of life. He is an unashamed romantic to whom the world of officialdom, professorialism and commercialism is quite foreign. The poet belongs to the world of naïve and the individual, to the world of children and women—even to the world of fools—for he shares with these the direct experience of "das Chaos der Bilderwelt" ("the chaos of the world of images"). Hence his constant longing for the night, the Eternal Mother, the symbol of death, for the night transports him again to the dreamworld of childhood. His quest after the grail of inward harmony led therefore along the path of sensual experience. Truth was a woman to be coveted, wooed and won. The joys and sorrows of life were wines to be drunk to the dregs. A Nietzschean affirmation of existence, therefore, but with none of his aristocratic scorn, a Faustian immersion in the stream of life, with no curb on appetite and no rein on impulse, an aesthetic amoralism—this is the faith which has sprung from his earlier adolescent romanticism. His awareness of the dualism in his own life is most clearly stated in the poem "An den Indischen Dichter Bhartrihari" ("To the Indian Poet Bhartrihari"), whom he hails as a kindred spirit, condemned like himself to pass "im Zickzack zwischen Trieb und Geist durchs Leben"—"Bald Mönch, bald Wüstling, Denker bald, bald Ticr" ("through life in a zigzag between desire and spirit"—"Now monk, now libertine, thinker now, now animal"). He sees his own life as an adventurous course from ascetic peaks to voluptuous depths, as the masculine and feminine parts of his nature in turn held sway. And if he has lingered longer in the valleys than on the mountain tops, that is the will of God—the will of the God immanent in himself and in nature around him. This conception that good and evil are both part of God goes beyond Christian morality and forms another tributary of that stream of German mysticism which had its source in Jakob Böhme.

This amoral acceptance of good and evil, joy and sorrow, leads Hesse to the conclusion that life is its own justification. Life is a flame to be nourished, a pilgrimage to be continually renewed—for only routine kills ("Die Flamme," "Stufe," "Bekenntnis") ("The Flame," "Step," "Confession"). "Atmen tut wohl, Atmen ist Seligkeit,/Ist Gebet und Gesang" ("To breathe is good, to breathe is bliss/It is a prayer and a song"), he cries, as the shadows of tomorrow fall across the path of today. And just as Goldmund, at the sight of a woman in labor, had realized that mankind's greatest joys and deepest pains often wear the same expression, so Hesse speaks of the intoxication of suffering and calls sorrows his sisters. This acceptance of life in all its forms finds its most emphatic expression in the poems "An die Freunde in schwerer Zeit," "Verzückung" and "Gang im Spätherbst" ("To Friends in a

Difficult Time," "Delight," "Walk in Late Autumn"), tl
formulates this mystical hedonism in the confession:

> Was ist mir Frucht? Was ist mir Ziel!—Ich blühte,
> Und Blühen war mein Ziel. Nun welk ich,
> Und Welken ist mein Ziel, nichts andres . . .
> Gott lebt in mir, Gott stirbt in mir, Gott leidet
> In meiner Brust, das ist mir Ziel genug.
> Weg oder Irrweg, Blüte oder Frucht,
> Ist alles eins, sind alles Namen nur.

> (What is fruit to me? What is a goal to me!—I bloomed,
> And blooming was my goal. Now I wither,
> And withering is my goal, nothing else . . .
> God lives in me, God dies in me, God suffers
> In my breast, that is enough goal for me.
> Right path or wrong, blossom or fruit,
> It is all one, they are only names.)

Only rarely does Hesse abandon this unquestioning approval of the whole complex web of being to wrestle with the problems of a synthesis. In the longer poem, "Media in Vita," however, whose free-verse form recalls the supple dignity of his prose, he sets out to diagnose the causes of man's fragmentariness and to prescribe a philosophy of life which will restore him to a whole. Whatever path we choose in life, he says, we are always teased with alternative paths: Love, that "Urwald der Lust" ("Jungle of Desire"), lures with the promise of a divine bliss but leads to an orgy of degradation; possession of wealth is fine and so is the scorn of wealth; art draws a veil over death and suffering and turns chaos to harmony; intellect makes man the hub of the universe, traces his lineage back to the primeval slime, lights up the dark porches of instinct and reveals the world and God as man's most sublime dream. So man snatches at each color in turn in the kaleidoscope of living and can only hold each for a moment. And even in the grave he is but a guest, being spewed out into the eternal flux of birth. The only way of life which does not finally disillusion is the inward life of the mystic. This mystical inwardness as an antidote to the dualism of living is confirmed in the later poems "Besinnung" ("Contemplation") (1933) and "Nachtgedanken" ("Night Thoughts") (1938). In both man is again portrayed as a shuttlecock of the masculine and the feminine, and no longer in these maturer works does the poet advocate a complete surrender to nature, the "Eternal Feminine" of his youth. On the contrary, the "Eternal Masculine," the Platonic world of the spirit, now becomes the focusing points of man's sublimest longings:

Göttlich ist und ewig der Geist.
Ihm entgegen, dessen wir Bild und Werkzeug sind,
Führt unser Weg; unsre innerste Sehnsucht ist:
Werden wie Er, leuchten in Seinem Licht!   ("Besinnung")

(Divine and eternal is the spirit.
Toward him, whose image and instrument we are,
Our way leads; our innermost longing is:
To become as He, to shine in His light!)   ("Contemplation")

But few are able, like Narcissus, to reach this state of grace, this total immersion in a spiritual ecstasy which leaves all bodily promptings behind like an empty chrysalis. For all those who are torn between the two poles of nature and the spirit, there is but one remedy: the miracle of love—not only the personal love of man for woman but above all the humanitarian love of man for man. Self-dedication to humanity, says Hesse—and it is the mission he himself has chosen—heals the elemental rift in man and leads from chaos to harmony. Only through love was the gulf between Narcissus and Goldmund crossed.

The general trend of Hesse's poems from youth to age is therefore from the external to the internal, from the world to self. But this is really only a change of emphasis: there can be no real separation of world and self, God and self. For the summary of his life's quest for truth, expressed in one of his shortest and serenest poems, bearing the significant title "Weg nach Innen" ("Way Within"), postulates a Goethean synthesis:

Wer den Weg nach innen fand,
Wer in glühndem Sichversenken
Je der Weisheit Kern geahnt,
Dass sein Sinn sich Gott und Welt
Nur als Bild und Gleichnis wähle:
Ihm wird jedes Tun und Denken
Zwiegespräch mit seiner eignen Seele,
Welche Welt und Gott enthält.

(He who found the way within,
Who in glowing introspection
Ever sensed the core of wisdom,
That his senses chose God and world
As image merely and metaphor:
For him every deed and thought
Becomes a dialogue with his own soul,
Which encompasses world and God.)

Hesse, like Gottfried Keller, is first and foremost a novelist whose poems take their place in the margin of his complete works. Poetry is for him recreation rather than purpose, so that occasional poems and *divertimenti* take up a disproportionate part of the whole. But even if some of the poems make promises which they do not keep, the poet himself never loses sight of his mission: he is a custodian of the spiritual and cultural values of the past and the protagonist of those values in the present. In the poems alone we can trace the roots of Hesse's humanism in Greece and Rome, in Christian and Indian mysticism and in European culture from Bach to Chopin and from the Italian Renaissance to Hölderlin and Nietzsche. He lashes the modern world unsparingly for its scientific rationalism, its unfeeling intellectualism, for its worship of the machine, whose logical masculinity is insensitive to dream, fantasy, music and love. In one of his last and saddest poems, "Orgelspiel" ("Organ Concert"), the poet laments the triumph of nihilism in the youth of his day. In an empty cathedral, pulsed around with the fever of commercialism, an aged organist is playing the same toccatas and fugues which have been played there down the centuries, but which to this age are meaningless symbols, a dead language; for beauty and culture are ebbing slowly away from our age with the old who alone cherish them. Whilst modern youth "schlingt und zehrt und hurrt sich durch die grellen/ Jahrmarktsfreuden ihrer Kinderwelt" ("engulfs, consumes and hurries itself through the shrill/Carnival joys of their children's world"), the poet must defy the scorn of the marketplace and stand fast as the guardian of those treasures that do not rust. In his poems, therefore, as in his greater epic works, Hesse poses the riddle of our age, and when he answers it, he answers it with the conviction of one who, as sensualist, humanist, romantic and mystic, has tested every possible answer in the conflicts of his own life. As long as there remain men like Hermann Hesse to diagnose and prescribe for the ills of our age, then there is still some hope of recovery.

Peter Heller

The Writer in Conflict with His Age: A Study in the Ideology of Hermann Hesse

Hermann Hesse's work extends over more than half a century. The present essay does not deal primarily with the views of the early "esthete" or with the creator of *Peter Camenzind* (1904), with the Hesse of *Unterm Rad* (*Beneath the Wheel*) (1905) or of *Rosshalde* (1914). We are concerned with the problematic author of the twenties and thirties who explored the depths of the psyche and confronted what he felt to be the desperate and chaotic aspects of his age, with the Hesse of *Demian* (1919), *Siddhartha* (1922), *Kurgast* (*Guest at the Spa*) (1924–25), of *Der Steppenwolf* (1927), of *Narcissus and Goldmund* (1930), of *Die Morgenlandfahrt* (*Journey to the East*) (1932), and *Das Glasperlenspiel* (*The Glass Bead Game*) (1943). As the title of this essay indicates, we shall inquire into Hesse's views concerning the relation between the writer and his age. Since our topic is theoretical in nature, the aim of the inquiry is to establish Hesse's ideological position rather than to evaluate the esthetic qualities or the artistic symbols which characterize his fiction and his poetry.[1]

[1] For details of reference, cf., A. Lemp's bibliography in: Max Schmid, *Hermann Hesse. Weg und Wandlung* (Leipzig und Zürich: Fretz und Wasmuth, 1941). Note the following abbreviations: B (*Betrachtungen,* Berlin: S. Fischer, 1928); BC (*Blick ins Chaos,* Bern: Verlag Seldwyla, 1922); DG (*Dank an Goethe,* Zürich: W. Classen, 1946); G (*Die Gedichte,* Zürich: Fretz und Wasmuth, 1942); GB (*Gedenkblätter,* Zürich: Fretz und Wasmuth, 1946); KF (*Krieg und Frieden. Betrachtungen zu Krieg und Politik seit dem Jahr 1914* , Zürich: Fretz und Wasmuth, 1946); KG (*Kurgast,* Berlin: S. Fischer, 1925); NR (*Die Nürnberger Reise,* Berlin: S. Fischer, 1927); ST ("Traktat vom Steppenwolf" in: *Der Steppenwolf,* Zürich: Manesse, 1930; the "Traktat" is contained in the novel and separately numbered); T (*Traumfährte,* Zürich: Fretz und Wasmuth, 1945); WM (*Eine Bibliothek der Weltliteratur,* Zürich: W. Classen, 1946).

Reprinted from Monatshefte, *vol. 46 (1954) by permission of the publisher.*

REALITY

For Hesse the drama, the sublime tragedy, and the genuine achievements of man take place in an inner realm. He likes to attack external reality as the one thing to which we should pay least attention. "Reality is annoying enough. It is always present while . . . more beautiful things . . . of which we have greater need, require our attention and care. . . . Reality is shabby and dreary. It always disappoints us. The only way to change reality is to deny it and to show that we are stronger than it" (T, 117). And yet this "refuse of life" defeats the efforts of the poet. He can accept the eternal contradictions and encompass the irreconcilable opposites, but he can do so only in his writings. How strange and frightening! Of all the sublime insights, of all the noble and magnificent sentiments which we find in their works, the artists—almost all of them—could transfer nothing or very little into the realities of their own lives (B, 91). If they could practice their wisdom they would be paragons of humanity, eminently happy men, but they would not be artists. They would have no reason to inflict upon themselves the complicated labor of creative work (B,187 f.).

Hesse confesses that he has known many hours when he longed to be normal (B, 91) and to share reality with the well-adjusted. Why did the common pursuits and pleasures of life have no stronger hold upon him? Neither business, nor family, nor even women could dispel his disgust. He could neither eat nor digest, neither sleep nor stay awake (G, 361 f.). Like an old beggar who condemns the age, he turned the barrel organ of his verse, envious of the dancers and the saxophones.[2] To be a writer was to practice a useless and dishonest profession. It was good to listen to those who proved the futility of Hesse's creative attempts (NR, 115). For he was but a shabby lone wolf, one of the family of schizophrenics just gifted enough and sufficiently harmless to be in no need of internment (KG, 13).

Hesse's attack on the world is never without self-irony. It is always linked to the author's need of vindicating his existence as a writer before the tribunal of his own conscience (B, 91). Again and again, Hesse is constrained to reestablish his own faith in the mission of the artist.

The immortals of the past, Hesse asserts, had all been strange, suffering, and complicated people. Disgust with reality was at the very root of their creative power. Were they, then, merely poor neurasthenics? Was it better to be a good citizen, a taxpayer, to raise children and to do business? If factories, cars and offices were the really normal things, why build museums, why collect and guard and exhibit these toys of ailing

[2]H. Hesse, *Krisis* (Berlin: S. Fischer, 1928), pp. 29 f., 38.

artists? Or did this tomfoolery, this nonsensical hocus-pocus contain, after all, something essential? Did it reveal something of the meaning and true value of human existence? And why were the railroad stations, the tenements and warehouses, why were all the creations of our utilitarian age so hideous and hopeless, fit only to nauseate a man and to persuade him to suicide? Was Hesse, the crazy poet, really crazy and sick because he failed to adjust to the way things happened to be? No, answered Hesse, it was better by far to suffocate and to die in this world of ours than to approve of it (NR, 96). And yet, the very rigor of this answer suggests that the poet is caught in a vicious circle in which each self-justification gives rise to new self-accusations.

THE PHILISTINES

Hesse seems least embarrassed by self-doubt in his condemnation of complacent mediocrity. He can sympathize, so he claims, with the saint and with the libertine, but not with the man who timidly lives between both. As antipode of the genius, the bourgeois shuns the extremes of self-dedication. He will never consent to his own annihilation. He wants to serve God, but he also likes a little intoxication. He wants to be virtuous, but he also would like some fun. He tries to settle down in a lukewarm intermediary zone, in a sphere of wholesome moderation. At the expense of intensity he attains security. Instead of being possessed with God, he has his peace of conscience. Instead of the delights and ecstasies of the spirit or of the flesh, he reaps comfort and enjoys conveniences which he prizes more than his inner freedom (ST, 18–20).

Throughout Hesse's writings the compromise of the bourgeois appears as the negative correlate to that synthesis of opposites which is the author's ideal. The Philistine settles at a level low enough to evade all vital and spiritual conflicts. Through his extraversion and materialism, through his observance of conventions, and through his obedience to superannuated laws, through his worship of power, and through his subservience to official institutions, he kills both spirit and soul.

The Philistine attempts to thwart the development of the artist. He gladly pays his respect to the established celebrities, but the wish to become a poet he considers an absurdity and a disgrace. Thus all figures, all efforts which transcend the commonplace are praised by textbooks and teachers only after they have become innocuous and a matter of the past. With respect to aspirations and actions here and now, the Philistine pedagogues—so it seemed to Hesse as a student—conspired to prevent the young generation from growing into fine, free men (T, 98). The world in its inertia is set against the daring and independence of genius. Hence every growing artist must choose once in his life between the values of the Philistines and the ideals of his own, between art and profit (GB, 13).

In his daily life, in his vices and virtues, the artist dramatizes his antagonism to the ordinary, dull, and conscientious citizen. ''People who perform regular and organized work . . . who attend to their pleasures with watch in hand, have no idea in what a lazy, irregular, moody, time-wasting fashion a poet spends his dubious existence. . . . No superior, no office, no ruling tells me when I have to get up in the morning and when I have to go to bed at night. . . . No deadline is set for my work, and it is nobody's business whether a poem of three stanzas takes me an afternoon or three months'' (NR, 17 ff.). In contrast to Mann, whose insistence on work, discipline, thoroughness, and sobriety conveys a sympathy with bourgeois virtues, Hesse consciously emphasizes the inspired irresponsibility of the artist to indicate his opposition to the ways of the Philistine. ''My waste of time [is] . . . not merely the result of laziness and disorder. It is also a conscious protest against the maddest and most sacred motto of the modern world, against the sentence 'Time is money' '' (NR, 21).

However, Hesse would concede that he is not altogether consistent in his campaign against the Philistines. In his opinion, most intellectuals and artists cannot completely dissociate themselves from the bourgeoisie. They form the considerable group of outsiders who, as individuals, have developed far beyond the bourgeois. They know the ecstasy of meditation as well as the gloomy joys of hatred and self-hatred. They are contemptuous of virtue, law, and common sense. And yet out of some weakness or inertia they cannot take the leap into the free, wild space of the universe. They cling with infantile sentiments to the heavy maternal body of the bourgeoisie. They resign or compromise, they despise the bourgeoisie and yet they are part of it, and strengthen and glorify it. In order to live, they must affirm mediocrity. Frequently esteemed by the Philistines for their great talents, these individuals fall short of perfection. They do not reach the heights of the truly tragic, but in the hell of their calamities their gifts mature and become fertile (ST, 21–23).

The highest place in Hesse's hierarchy is reserved to the greatest sufferer, to the man who lives in complete defiance of the Philistines. ''The word tragic, that . . . mystical word which has come down to us from . . . the mythical youth of mankind . . . signifies nothing else but the fate of the hero who perishes because he follows his own stars in defiance of the accepted laws.'' His fate reveals to mankind again and again the knowledge of its innermost being. For the tragic hero demonstrates to the millions of cowards that disobedience to man-made rules is no act of crude wilfulness but loyalty to a higher and more sacred law. The herd demands of everybody adjustment and subordination.

However, its highest honors are not granted to the patient and docile but to the few who are stubborn, who follow their inner voice and remain true to their own mind (KF, 132 f.).

The Philistine fears nothing more than self-discovery. Yet to become aware of one's innermost nature, to strive towards it, to live in harmony with it, to possess it, constitutes the one and only valid goal of human existence. Real progress is possible only when men find the courage to live their own fate. All literature has but the purpose to point the way to the real self (HG, 273). For "the kingdom of God is within you" (HB, 59).

POLITICS AND SOCIAL CHANGE

This faith afforded the basis for Hesse's hostility to his age and his public. For, unlike Mann, he has retained his aversion to politics, to public affairs, and indeed, to all larger social intercourse throughout his entire career.

What could politics be to the man who felt the courage to be himself? He cared neither for monarchy nor for democracy, neither for revolutionaries nor for conservatives. His was a sacred egotism. He valued only the mysterious power of life within him, which neither money nor external power nor any other of the substitutes and inventions born of self-distrust could preserve or intensify (KF, 136 f.).

Even in the instances in which Hesse seems to grant that politics can be more than a product of greed and ambition, he assigns to the politicians a place far below the artist and thinker. The politicians think that with electoral reforms and the like they are the makers of progress. In reality, they lag centuries behind and merely attempt to translate into practice on a small scale one or the other of the presentiments and thoughts of the spiritual men (B, 90).

The poet knows that human lives cannot be reduced to arithmetical problems. To him, the calculations of the economists are empty fantasies. For him, there exist neither the fates of capitalism nor those of socialism. He can offer no program to the young generation. He can only tell them that "action never came from one who had asked before, 'What am I to do?' Action is like the light that bursts forth from a goodly sun. . . . It cannot be hatched out in the brain or decided upon by hairsplitting" (KF, 157).

Though Hesse—after the First World War—seemed convinced that the overwhelming majority of his fellow men were hopelessly immature, he addressed German youth as if it formed a congregation of potential saints or supermen. Every one of them was to be "strong and true to himself, trusting in nobody but himself and in the fortune which favors the strong and the bold'' (KF, 188). Actually, Hesse's message, though couched in the ambiguous and aggressive pathos of Nietzschean diction, was one of peace, goodwill, and acceptance of the situation in which the *Reich* found itself in 1918.

Curiously enough, the lack of positive orientation implicit in Hesse's general aversion to public affairs never prevented him from forming clear-cut and consistent opinions on the specific political issues of the day.

The period of the First World War, Hesse wrote, was great only for those to whom the experience of death and danger brought for the first time a breath of inner life (KF, 105 f.). The poets needed no such reminder. Dedicated to true human values, they had to protest against the organized madness which destroyed all intellectual integrity and denied the unity of European culture (DG, 14 f.). "Irresponsible scribbling, some of it inspired by enthusiastic intoxication and some of it simply bought, became the order of the day. . . . Even famous scholars and authors all of a sudden wrote like sergeant majors. The bridge between the spirit and the people seemed to have been destroyed, in fact, it seemed as if the spirit had ceased to be'' (DG, 13). In that period the ''men who lived outside the world'' and who warned against the insane recklessness of political and military leaders were no longer considered mere poets but were branded as defeatists, grumblers, and enemies of the fatherland (KF, 104 f.).

Hesse spent the years of the First World War in Switzerland, engaged in a book service for prisoners of war. He was equally opposed to the killing and to the bureaucratization brought about by the war. The authorities, he felt, stifled all individual life. In this respect his wartime experience appeared to Hesse as a repetition of his experiences at school. The authorities led men to murder one another without cause (KF).

In spite of his aversion to mass society and his antipolitical bias, Hesse—always antiauthoritarian and deeply concerned with the unhampered development of the individual—was led to assume the position of a democratic progressive. Though hunger, poverty, red flags, the republic, and popular enthusiasm were not the ''truly 'great' things'' (KF, 107), Hesse hoped the Weimar democracy would prove a turning point in German history.

In the eighteenth and early nineteenth centuries Germany had cultivated the inwardness of poetry, music, and philosophy. With the rise to power and material wealth, Germany had lost its soul. Total defeat could lead to a rediscovery of the nation's real self. While the Germans could not return to small peaceful towns and compose poetry or play sonatas (KF, 118), the people could now gain independence and maturity. Once again Germany might enrich the world by a steady, quiet stream of warmth and thoughtfulness (KF, 111).

As the promise of Weimar failed and Germany turned toward National Socialism, Hesse, a naturalized Swiss citizen, became increasingly pessimistic. A compromise with the tenets and practices of the Nazis had always been out of the question for him. By 1938 he felt that the machine of the modern state—"the machinery for making money and for waging wars into which the world has turned"—must smash itself to pieces before enduring new creations would become possible. And yet the poet must strive to preserve "the life of the soul" or, at least, the longing for it. We must play "our little flutes" amidst the noise of cannons and loudspeakers. We must accept the fact that this activity seems quite hopeless and, indeed, ridiculous. This must be "our form of bravery."[3]

Germany's betrayal of her mission and the lack of soul in the entire modern world was brought about, according to Hesse, chiefly by the industrial revolution, that "strange transformation" of men and things engendered like a disease from the smoke of the first steam engines (KF, 112). For the poet the factory is the symbol of the chase after money, of slavery, and sinister imprisonment (G, 297). Hesse dreams of liberating man by wrecking the stupid, malicious machines which are so utterly devoid of "folly, and love, dream, music, and imagination" (G, 317). Characteristically, the *Morgenlandfahrer (Traveler to the East)* and Hesse himself avoid all modern means of transportation. His manner of traveling, Hesse declared, remained approximately on the level of the Middle Ages (NR, 24).

This antitechnological bias and the revulsion from everything that went under the name of Americanism did not prevent the poet from realizing that mechanization could not be stopped. "As a romantic, as an infantile soul who always turns toward the past," he confessed his love for the Tessin, for its winding rivers, its woods which lacked rational cultivation, for the decaying roadside shrines and the primitive fireplaces. He is fond of these remaining vestiges of the past, the delicate, old, and somewhat helpless things, and of the faces and gestures of old country folk which have the same childlike, pious, and heartfelt qualities. He regrets the living flood of changes and innovations. He dislikes the straight-edged riverbeds, the new highways, and every iron pole conducting electricity, but he knows that everywhere the old world must come to an end, everywhere money will triumph over custom and rational economy will oust the idyl. Nonetheless, Hesse claims, the basic conflict is not between progress and romanticism but between the exter-

[3]H. Hesse, *Briefe* (Berlin-Frankfurt: Suhrkamp, 1951), p. 187.

nal, the superficial, and the inward man. At heart, the poets do not protest against money and reason, they do not condemn the railroads and
automobiles but the increasing shallowness of the human soul. At heart,
the poet knows that his lack of enterprise and business sense corresponds
to the lack of a psychological dimension in his antipode, the businessman
and seeker of profit. ''Our romantic and poetic immaturity is no more infantile than the childish and proud self-confidence of the world-conquer-
ing engineer who believes in his slide rule as we believe in our God, and
who is seized with anger or fear when the exclusive validity of his laws is
shaken by Einstein.'' Let the literati of the big cities mock at the sen-
timentalists! ''Some of us . . . have more faith in the future
and . . . yearn for it more fervently than do many of those who believe in
the religion of progress. For we believe in the transitory nature of the
machine and in the eternity of God.''[4]

According to Hesse, the writer cannot sympathize with the extraversion of the industrial age, with the approach from the outside, and with
the habit of thinking purely in terms of matter-of-fact. However, he is
fascinated by the destructive and chaotic forces of our epoch. To the
postwar Hesse the descent into the depth of the unconscious and the
disintegration of traditional norms appeared as the necessary condition
for rejuvenation and for a new self-awareness. ''The quiet, gentle,
somewhat boring temple of European art . . . has been invaded by the
painted skulls, the hairy dance masks, the terrifying chimaeras of primitive peoples and ages.'' This victorious, splendid invasion is evidently a
sign of decline, but of a ''healthy'' decline which is at the same time the
beginning of a rebirth. It is due to a weariness in the functions of an
overrefined organism. The souls of individuals and nations are striving
toward an opposite pole (B,97).

Hesse approved of the expressionists because they attempted to give
direct expression to their inner upheaval. He encouraged the writing of
''bad'' poems which were nothing but self-expression, nothing but
Schrei and *Entladung* (B, 97, 99). At the same time he was convinced
that such products were not truly artistic. The entire literature of his age
was torn between the demand for ruthless confession and the demand for
the perfection of form (NR, 79). The contemporary poet must needs
oscillate between chaos and tradition.

According to Hesse, the last great period of German literature was
the epoch of classicism and romanticism, the age up to 1850. Even where
they no longer express our feelings and problems, the works of Goethe,
Hölderlin, Kleist, of Jean Paul, Brentano, Hoffmann, Eichendorff, and
Stifter are always perfect and complete as artistic creations (NR, 78).

[4]H. Hesse, *Bilderbuch. Schilderungen* (Berlin: S. Fischer, 1926), p. 223 ff.

"The German letters of our time—though interesting and full of problematic issues—are an ephemeral and desperate affair" (NR, 77). This
verdict includes Hesse's own writings. Nowadays, he claims, the attempts to form genuine artistic works always reveal a trace of the
stereotype, the presence of a model which has become lifeless and unreal
(NR, 77). Tempting as it is, the endeavor to imitate the classics is futile.
Hence Hesse could not enjoy, or approve of, many contemporary books
written in a beautiful and solid manner. "The literature of an age of
transition, a literature which has become problematic and unsure of itself,
has a function and value insofar as the writers attempt to confess with the
utmost sincerity their own problems, their own misery, and the problems
and misery of their time" (NR, 77 f.). Yet even for those who are ready
for extreme candor to the point of self-surrender, the problem arises how
to escape the tradition (NR, 79). "Where shall we find an adequate
idiom? . . . The language of our books and our schools is of no help.
The character of our written style has been moulded a long time ago.
Isolated and desperate works such as Nietzsche's *Ecce Homo* seemed to
point a way. In the end they showed us only more clearly that there was
none. Psychoanalysis appeared as a remedy and it brought some progress. Yet to this time, no author, neither a psychoanalyst nor a poet
trained in psychoanalysis, has freed this sort of psychology of its academic armor, its shell of narrowness, dogmatism, and vanity" (NR,
79 f.).

The double allegiance to the old and to the new accounts for some of
Hesse's contradictions. He maintains, for example, that only a handful of
books can survive historical change and are worthy to endure. Yet he
deplores the disappearance of the editions of lesser authors of the German
classical period as one of the most disturbing and ugliest symptoms of
our terrible age (WM, 91). Since the gates to the temple of true poetry
were closed (T, 118 f.), Hesse conceived of himself at times as a guardian
of the heritage, as a humble typesetter who loyally persevered in his
service to the word (T, 50). Indeed, the entire hierarchy of *Das Glasperlenspiel (The Glass Bead Game)* serves the preservation of cultural
traditions. And yet the same author who protested against the return to the
Middle Ages, who abhorred the vulgarity of our age, its unprecedented
brutality and barbarism, its lack of all aesthetic forms, and its disintegration of ethical standards, would tell the young generation in the words of
Nietzsche that they must wring the neck of a collapsing pseudo-culture
and begin anew (B,158 f.). The dignity of traditions, the dignified poet,
the sanctity of art had become mere fictions. It was futile to struggle
against the complete decay and disappearance of literature (T, 38 f.). We
should let literature die in peace (cf. T, 118 f.).

THE WRITER AND HIS PUBLIC

Hesse's attitude toward contemporary literature, toward his age, and toward the external world in general implies a problematic relationship between writer and public. A poet who "deep in his heart doubts himself and the value of his poetic efforts" stands before an audience of Philistines with whom, he feels, he has nothing in common. Ideally speaking, Hesse comments, such a confrontation could only end either in the self-annihilation of the poet or in his being stoned by his listeners. However, in the empirical world there is room for a "shabby adjustment" (NR, 81).

Hesse frequently expressed the utmost contempt for his profession, and indeed for the entire cultural and intellectual industry. "Lord," he exclaimed, "let me take part in some work which makes more sense . . . than this puppet show" (NR, 103). He claimed to hate his literary name and reputation (NR, 42 f.). He complained about the letters he received from his readers, about the offers made by publishers. He shunned all gatherings of celebrities. He abhorred the newspapers (GB, 118 f.). It would be bliss not to be reminded of literature constantly, not to be reminded that you belonged to a class and to a profession which was suspect and lacking decency and therefore held in low esteem (NR, 40). It would be bliss to be unreachable, not to be known, not to be a victim of the idiotic cult of personalities, not to be forced to live in that dirty, hypocritical, and stifling atmosphere of publicity. But there was no escape. The world was pitiless. It demanded from the poet not works and thoughts but his address and his person, to adore it and to throw it away again, to enjoy it and to spit at it as a naughty little girl does with her doll (NR, 40 ff.).

The fame of the great men of the past was far nobler, more solid, more innocent, and at the same time more venerable than our stylish celebrity. For the contemporary brand of fame had nothing to do with humans and their works. It was the short-lived glory of best sellers and literary fads (GB, 128).

Hesse continually insulted his public. Indeed, he regarded the poet's hostility toward his contemporaries as one of the forces which inspired modern writing (B, 48 f.). He declared that the Germans were particularly unresponsive. It was part of the German fate that the great spirits of this nation seemed to have no effect upon the people (B, 233). The lack of an adequate forum was responsible for the tragic destiny of the German writer, of the German spirit, and of the German language (DG, 13).

These sentiments seem to derive partly from Hesse's own experiences in World War I. The attacks he then suffered from the press, his sudden fall from grace, his keen disappointment with the German nation affected the author so deeply that he doubted whether he would "endure the test, whether he would not perish in the conflict" (KF, 11). He could never forget the insults inflicted upon him by the patriotic journalists of that era.

This sensitivity is characteristic of Hesse. Precisely because he had always lived on the brink of isolation, he experienced the temporary rejection as a shock. For it was in his writings that Hesse had most successfully bridged the gap between himself and the outside world. To be sure, after the war, after the public had prevented him from hiding behind a pseudonym (Emil Sinclair), he claimed that in order to revenge himself he would make an effort to write only the things which very few people can enjoy (NR, 41 f.). His life, he said, would become more peaceful through this exclusion of the masses. Actually, he continued his lively, if embittered, romance with a large and appreciative public. He did assume a more detached, suspicious, and contemptuous attitude in the postwar period of the twenties. Yet he was never to avoid publication like Kafka, not did he attempt to create a restricted circle as George had done at one time. He did not become an esoteric author. He increased his reputation. He was eminently successful as a prolific and representative writer.

The readers, in turn, experienced Hesse's railing at the public and his accusations of the dull bourgeoisie as part of an accepted pattern, Hesse's change of tone after the war merely increased the vehemence of this acceptable anti-Philistinism. A well-established romantic tradition demands of the poet a show of indifference and even of contempt. The public itself desired of literature relief from the routines and values of ordinary life. Even the assault on the Philistine is probably enjoyable to many Philistines, for they necessarily make up the majority of those who read so successful a book as *Steppenwolf*. Hesse's numerous readers identified themselves with the lonely creative type rather than with the dull average. It would have never occurred to the public to protest against the treatment it received in Hesse's works.

On first sight, it might seem as if Hesse denied the vital relationship between the writer and his audience, just as he seemed to deny the contact between the writer and his age. Actually, he is both concerned with his public and aware of the writer's function as the representative of his age. Hesse thrives on contradictions. He assigns the writer a realm essentially outside of history, but he also defines the writer as the man who takes upon himself the common burden, as the prophet who interprets his private sorrows in terms of public significance.

A prophet is a sick man. He lacks the essence of bourgeois virtue. He does not possess the . . . beneficial instinct of self-preservation. . . . [However, he] has a strange, pathological, and divine capacity. . . . He possesses esoteric knowledge, he is one of the initiated. That is to say, in this man, a given people or an age, a country or a continent have developed an organ capable of tremendous suffering, an infinitely sensitive and precious antenna. . . . The "pathological" character whom we have in mind reinterprets the movements of his soul in such a manner that they refer to the universally human. Every man has visions, emotions, and dreams. Every man possesses imagination. On the way which leads from the unconscious to consciousness, every vision, every dream, every notion, every thought can be interpreted in a thousand different ways, and each of these interpretations can be correct. The seer and prophet does not interpret his visions in a personal manner. The incubus that oppresses him does not remind him of his personal sickness or of his own death, but of the disease and the death of the entire entity for whom he serves as organ and antenna. This entity can be a family, a party, a people, It can also be the whole of mankind. (BC, 184)

The concept of the poet as a representative sufferer is related to the idea that the genius experiences his own fate in such a form that his *vita* becomes symbolic of the historical events and problems of the age. Hesse describes his life and his sufferings in stages which run parallel to the stages in the European crisis (T, 111 f.). To suffer with the age is a sign of distinction (B, 71, 99).

It is fitting that an admirer of Hesse, Fritz Strich, interpreted the author's own career in terms of a representative isolation. Hesse's loneliness, Strich asserted, was a symbol for all who lived in this age of atomization. "All of us wander about in the same desert, but only the poet endowed with the gift of song can say what he suffers, what we suffer. In speaking of himself, he speaks for us."[5]

[5]Fritz Strich, *Der Dichter und die Zeit* (Bern: A. Francke, 1947), p. 380 f.

Eugene F. Timpe

Hermann Hesse in the United States

Subsequent to Hermann Hesse's death the *New York Times* carried an obituary notice with the statement that ''To American readers he remained largely unapproachable, despite a flurry of interest in his novels after the award of the Nobel Prize.''[1] Had such a notice been written even a few years earlier, the word *unapproachable* would very likely been replaced by *unknown*. In 1957, on Hesse's eightieth birthday, a contributor to *The Saturday Review* dejectedly noted that the event would produce no celebrations in America like those held in his honor in other parts of the world.[2] Nine years earlier another commentator observed that any controversy in America similar to that heated one which took place in Europe over Hesse's being awarded the Nobel Prize would be precluded simply by our ignorance of him; following that pronouncement, the author considered it appropriate to offer an elementary introduction to Hesse, his life, and his works.[3] Up to the last decade, as a matter of fact, such basic approaches to Hesse not only were necessary but commonplace, so little was he known. Heavily dependent upon platitudes, they ordinarily began with a few generalizations, continued with biography, and concluded with summaries of his works—eloquent but mute testimony to the obscurity in America of the man recognized in other lands as ''the dean of contemporary German literature.''[4] In 1946, *Time* magazine, prodded into its first acknowledgment of Hesse, *twenty-three years* after he was first introduced to American readers, printed a

[1] 10 August 1962, p.19.
[2] Claude Hill, Review of *Journey to the East*, XL (1 June 1957), 12–13.
[3] Marion Foran, ''Hermann Hesse,'' *Queens Quarterly,* LV (9 May 1948), 180–189.
[4] Hill, *loc. cit.*

Reprinted from Symposium, *vol. 23 (1969), pp. 73–79, by permission of the publisher.*

short, condescending account of the fact that he had received the Nobel Prize. It is probably safe to say that the only one by the name of Hesse, or variant spelling thereof, commonly known in America before 1957 had the given name of Rudolf.

The dreary tale of Hesse's neglect in America prior to 1957 is revealed by statistics as well as by testimonials. Klaus W. Jonas' bibliography lists only eight articles on Hesse published in America by 1945.[5] By 1946 only four of his novels had been translated into English, and all four were out of print. After the awarding of the Nobel Prize, two of these were reissued and two new ones were added.[6] Except in two or three journals, none of his poems and shorter prose writings had been translated and printed.

Gratifying as it might be to assert that Hesse was applauded by the few even if spurned by the many, it would not be quite accurate to do so. When *Demian*, published in German in 1919, was translated into English in 1923, the reviewer for the *Boston Transcript* wrote, "We are confused (and perhaps exasperated) by so much talk of soul forces, shaping destinies, realizations of self. Whatever may have been the author's purpose, he gives us a nightmare of abnormality, a crazed dream of a paranoiac."[7] Reissuance of that same work twenty-five years later, supported by a laudatory foreword by Thomas Mann,[8] evoked the remarkable judgment that it "reveals, as few books have, the unapologetic philosophic origins of Germany's unquenchable thirst for the intoxicating waters of world domination."[9] *Steppenwolf*, translated in 1929, was regarded as "rather orgiastic and suggestive of organized and joyless vice" by one reviewer,[10] and as a "witch's broth" by another.[11] It was not until after the advent of *The Glass Bead Game* and the Nobel Prize that the general tone of the reviews became more approving, and with the latest translation of *Demian*, published in 1965, it became, comparatively speaking, almost euphoric. But this development did not take place until the end of almost three decades of neglect.

If fame is also a product, much like Taine's sugar, vice, and vitriol,

[5] "Hermann Hesse in Amerika. Bibliographie," *Monatshefte*, XLIV (1952), 95–99. For a continuation of Jonas's bibliography, see his "Additions to the Bibliography of Hermann Hesse," *Papers of the Bibliographical Society of America*, XLIX (1955), 358–360.

[6] One major work, *Siddhartha*, first published in 1922, was not translated for twenty-nine years; another, *Die Morgenlandfahrt* (*Journey to the East*), was not translated until 1957, twenty-five years after its initial publication in Germany.

[7] Written by "W.A.N.," 14 April 1923, p. 5.

[8] Also published in *The Saturday Review*, XXXI (3 January 1948), 5–7.

[9] Emmett Dedmon, *Chicago Sun* (21 January 1948).

[10] L. P. Hartley, *The Saturday Review*, CXLVII (1 June 1929), 746.

[11] Anon., *Boston Transcript* (4 September 1929), 2.

admirers of Hesse are tempted to wonder just which of the ingredients were missing during the long period of apathy. Upon reflection, it is not difficult to suggest a few. To begin with, it is obvious that the timing was unfortuitous. Hesse's first works came out in America during a period in which German literature, after having been exceptionally well received in the first decade of the century, was entering upon a fifteen-year period of almost total eclipse.[12] Further, by the time his works finally began to reach our bookstores, the problems of the 1920's, secondary targets in some of his works, had been replaced by those of a different nature.[13] During those years, too, we were largely preoccupied by our own alter egos—Anderson, Dos Passos, Lewis, Dreiser, Sinclair, and Hemingway.[14] After all, as Claude Hill remarked, "We like our 'realities' strong and three-dimensional and full-flavored, and we are inclined to be bewildered by an author who scorns the 'shabby reality' of the material world."[15] It is no wonder that Hesse was ignored not only by the public but also by the czars of the book clubs, those purveyors of popularity who might have done so much to bring him before the public.

To discover another obstacle one need not search very far; one need only read Hesse in English and it becomes immediately apparent that he was not well served by his early translators. One cannot explain why; one can only wonder that a stylist as complex as Mann, a poet as esoteric as Rilke, and a novelist as abstruse as Kafka seemed to offer no unsurmountable obstacles to translation, while Hesse, writing in a relatively simple and traditional idiom, apparently presented great difficulties.[16] And perhaps this problem of translation helps to explain why no selection of his shorter prose works was published, which by itself would have done much toward introducing him to American readers; although it is indeed a fact that Hesse himself discouraged such an undertaking—he called it a "homeopathic Hesse"—on the grounds that it would reflect his ideas inaccurately through the omission of those parts of his total work which any judicious editor would consider controversial.[17]

[12] B. Q. Morgan, "Preface," *A Critical Bibliography of German Literature in English Translation*, 2nd ed. (Stanford, 1938).

[13] Stanley R. Townsend, "Die moderne deutsche Literatur in Amerika," *Die Sammlung*, V (May 1954), 237–243.

[14] Felix Anselm, "Hermann Hesse," *Poet Lore*, LIII (1947), 353–360.

[15] Hill, *loc. cit.*

[16] In evaluating a translation of *Das Glasperlenspiel* (*The Glass Bead Game*), Horst Frenz noted that "it contains so many errors that frequently the meaning of a sentence or a thought is completely distorted." "The Art of Translation," *Comparative Literature: Method and Perspective* (Carbondale, 1961), 82. W. LaMarr Kopp, in *Anglo-German and American-German Crosscurrents, III: German Literature in the United States, 1945–1960*

One of the most important reasons for our overlooking Hesse, however, was inherent within his own form of writing. He once said, "I know that I am not a story teller,"[18] and it is evident from his writings, especially those of his later period, that narration was often sacrificed to didacticism. He believed that "the true profession of man is to find his way to himself;"[19] and the search for this way became a metaphysical search, associated with and intensified by Oriental philosophy. The wisdom of the East was to broaden and strengthen the potentialities for self-realization within the human products of a declining Western civilization. If this was the way to self-discovery, it was not the way to popularity, at least not until recently. It brought him closer to Thoreau than to Hemingway, and it left him, the "poet of metaphysical twilight, Rembrandt of the word,"[20] open to the charge of perpetuating a form of romanticism.[21] *Time* magazine, in a typical "Timeism," called him "relentlessly esoteric—one of those Faustian fellows who make Moholes out of moleholes."[22] Certainly, his themes, as well as the melancholy, mandarin quality of the heroes which they evoked, were not to the taste of American readers of the Jazz Age, the Great Depression, and the war years.

Hesse's American revival began in 1957. Apparently it occurred more or less simultaneously on all fronts—publishing, popular, and academic. Since 1957 more than forty articles have been published on Hesse, in both scholarly and general journals. There began, also at that time, a sharp increase in the quantity of his works published. Whereas there had been a small flurry of interest in the late forties—*Demian* was reissued with Thomas Mann's foreword, *Steppenwolf* was reprinted in an old translation, and *Two Tales* was printed, no doubt for use as a classroom text—followed by a lesser output of his works during the period of relapse which preceded the age of the vogue; at the beginning of this new period six of his books were suddenly reissued, and by 1968

[18]Obituary notice, *New York Times* (10 August 1962), 19.

[19]*Ibid.*

[20]G. E. Mueller, "Hermann Hesse," *Books Abroad*, XXI (1947), 146–152, 287.

[21]Townsend, *loc. cit.*, and "The German Humanist Hermann Hesse," *Modern Language Forum*, XXXII (1947), 1–12.

[22]LXXXVI (30 July 1965), 68.

(Chapel Hill, 1967), p. 135, suggested that the problem was intensified because Hesse had neither "authorized" translator nor "official" publisher in America.

[17]J. Malthaner, "Visit with Hermann Hesse," *Books Abroad*, XXV (1951), 236–237.

almost all of his principal writings were in print, several in fresh translations.[23]

Both the tone and the subjects of the scholarly and popular studies on Hesse were improved. Based upon the assumption that the reader already knew something about Hesse, they dealt competently with his romanticism, his form and structure, his ideology, his heroes, his relationship to music, and even with his cat—one critic proved, bowing, perhaps, to the muse Thalia, that the inspiration for one of the characters in *Journey to the East* was Hesse's cat.[24] *Monatshefte* devoted an entire issue to Hesse in 1961, probably the single most concerted effort of the period, and to this we are indebted for some fine work on such subjects as the outsider concept, his chiliastic vision, the structure of *Beneath the Wheel*, some parallels between *Steppenwolf* and *Wilhelm Meister*, the death of Josef Knecht, Hesse's use of names, a comparison of *Wilhelm Meister* and *The Glass Bead Game*, Hesse's criticism of English and American literature, and his symbolism in "Heumond."

Establishing scholarly activity on the basis of numbers and kinds of articles and assessing popular interest on the basis of publishing records are very different matters from explaining such phenomena. To evolve an hypothesis one must desert the world of hard facts. Nothing, for example, short of a census of Hesse's present readers is likely to reveal why they think they are drawn to him, and nothing less than some kind of depth analysis of these same readers is likely to reveal why they really are. Both of these attempts would be subject to as many interpretations as there are ways of evaluating statistics and techniques for determining those subliminal matters which dictate personal taste. Without venturing upon such treacherous territory, however, it may be possible, on the basis of a safe assumption or two, to suggest an explanation.

The assumption basic to this explanation is that Hesse, for a variety of reasons, has appealed to two entirely different groups of readers. His first, basic, and most conventional appeal attracted only a few American readers in the past, although in Europe and elsewhere, notably in Japan, it was sufficient to create a vast reading public almost from the very beginning. That universal appeal, particularly evident in his earlier works, was not unlike that which was exerted by a number of popular novelists of the first part of the century, but it probably does little to explain the recent resurgence of interest in him during the past decade in America.

It is his second audience, attracted by many of his later works,

[23]*Steppenwolf* in 1957; *Demian* in 1965. Farrar, Straus & Giroux recently announced publication of *Narcissus and Goldmund*, soon to be followed by other major works.

[24]R. H. Farquharson, "The Identity and Significance of Leo in Hesse's *Morgenlandfahrt*," *Monatshefte*, LV (1963), 122–128.

especially those subsequent to *Demian*, which accounts for his recent American vogue. This is based upon Hesse as the author of mind-expanding works, works in which the emphasis has shifted from the palpable straightforward narration of events to a kind of subjectivism which is related to the search for self, mysticism, archetypal symbolism, logical paradox as psychological truth, and musical themes and forms which establish a liaison with the subconscious. These works seem not to have exerted their effects earlier simply because the audience to which they appeal, an audience with characteristics rather different from those of its counterpart of a generation ago, has only recently come into existence.

The first and most obvious characteristic of the audience is youthfulness. More than half of the population of the United States has been born since the end of World War II, and since this group, by virtue of its character and by authority of its mass, is evolving its own values, it has rejected, even more vehemently than youth always rejects, the beliefs, prejudices, and apathies of the preceding generation. Uninfluenced by their elders' rejection of Hesse, this group has largely accepted him, not only because of his appeal to youth in general, but also because of his appeal to those of this time and place.

The matter of a general appeal to youth is most obvious. It has always been in the nature of the young to revolt against the weight of tradition, nowadays called "the establishment," and Hesse's preoccupation with the awakening of spring and his almost inevitable depiction of the perennial revolt against authority offer a good deal with which to identify. As one student recently wrote in a class paper, "He writes about troubled people trying to maintain individuality in a society which forces conformity." They can see themselves as Goldmund or Demian in revolt against the father image and that which it symbolizes, or better yet, as Hans Giebenrath, subjected to "the system," forced into a mold, the spirit and intelligence crushed. They can even identify themselves with Harry Haller, insofar at least as he expresses the attempt to free himself from the constraints of conformity.

Not only has this rebellion been more intense of late by virtue of the high proportion of the population involved in it, but also it has differed somewhat from the usual youthful rebellion in ways which have made Hesse seem almost to be its prophet. Few of his works fail to express antipathy toward bourgeois materialism, and the new generation heartily seconds his motion against the apotheosis of prosperity. It joins him also in his rejection of conventional morality; although this may not have been one of his major themes, it was in his writings for those who sought it, and it is not difficult to imagine that from the point of view of many an undergraduate, Goldmund's trip along the high road exemplifies rather well the aspirations of the uncommitted. Not only are vagrancy and amorality part of the more excessive and divergent aspects of this revolt, but also even the use of narcotics, as in *Steppenwolf*, seems to have been approved by Hesse.

Conventional religious beliefs have apparently no more place in this brave new world than have absolute standards of morality. Certainly Hesse's religion was anything bur conventional. To utterances such as that made by a certain follower of Abraxas—''We should hold nothing forbidden which the soul in us desires''[25]—many youthful readers are ''tuned-in,'' and any seeker of self through Zen and Orientalism is likely to have read and admired *Siddhartha*. The religious attitudes of this group are, like Hesse's, part of the cult of self-discovery; and like Hesse's heroes, it finds reality not in exterior things but in itself. The result in both cases is an alienation from the mainstreams of tradition, and whether it be cause or result, it is apparent that the generation devoted to the search for itself has become self-conscious, self-modeling, and self-breeding. Like Hesse, in the search for inner resources leading to the expansion and intensification of life, it has ripened itself for mysticism.

Prompted by the doctrine of love and by a sense of insecurity, they sympathize with Hesse's intense humanism. They applaud his reverence for life, and even if his treatment of war was sometimes equivocal, they sense his pacifism and read it, as Harry Haller seems to have read the Tract, more for what they find in themselves than for what they find in it. As a matter of fact, there is even some danger that Hesse will become a kind of thesis author like Thoreau, with the consequent difficulty that it is not always possible to distinguish what his public finds *in* him from what they read *into* him. To those who have used Hesse's books in the classroom, it is evident that he, more than most authors, evokes the students' tendency to use the text as a justification for speaking about themselves. Perhaps it is this therapeutic quality most of all which attracts the new generation to Hesse. Not only does he endorse their own particular conflicts, but also he leads them through discovery of themselves back into the midst of a newly structured life in which they derive their own identities, create their own universe, and establish its order. For them, it is as Hesse said in *Demian*: ''We make gods, and we wrestle with them, and they bless us'' (p. 155).

[25]*Demian* (New York, 1923), p. 143.

Selected Bibliography

PRINCIPAL WORKS BY HERMANN HESSE
TRANSLATED INTO ENGLISH

Autobiographical Writings. Ed. T. Ziolkowski. Trans. Denver Lindley. New York: Farrar, Straus and Giroux, 1972.

Beneath the Wheel. Trans. M. Roloff and M. Lebeck. New York: Farrar, Straus and Giroux, 1968.

Demian. Trans. M. Roloff and M. Lebeck. New York: Harper and Row, 1965.

Gertrude. Trans. Hilda Rosner. New York: Farrar, Straus and Giroux, 1970.

The Glass Bead Game. (*Magister Ludi*). Trans. Richard and Clara Winston. New York: Holt, Rinehart and Winston, 1969.

If the War Goes On. . . . Trans. Ralph Manheim. New York: Farrar, Straus and Giroux, 1971.

The Journey to the East. Trans. Hilda Rosner. New York: Farrar, Straus and Giroux, 1956.

Klingsor's Last Summer. Trans. Richard and Clara Winston. New York: Farrar, Straus and Giroux, 1970.

Narcissus and Goldmund. Trans. Ursule Molinaro. New York: Farrar, Straus and Giroux, 1968.

Peter Camenzind. Trans. M. Roloff. New York: Farrar, Straus and Giroux, 1969.

Poems. Ed. and trans. James Wright. New York: Farrar, Straus and Giroux, 1970.

Reflections. Ed. Volker Michels. Trans. Ralph Manheim. New York: Farrar, Straus and Giroux, 1974.

Rosshalde. Trans. Ralph Manheim. New York: Farrar, Straus and Giroux, 1970.

Siddhartha. Trans. Hilda Rosner. New York: New Directions, 1951.

Steppenwolf. Trans. B. Creighton. Revised J. Mileck and H. Frencz. New York: Holt, Rinehart and Winston, 1963.

Stories of Five Decades. Ed. T. Ziolkowski. Trans. Ralph Manheim and
    Denver Lindley. New York: Farrar, Straus and Giroux, 1972.

SELECTED ARTICLES AND BOOKS ABOUT HESSE IN ENGLISH

Andrews, R. C. "The Poetry of Hermann Hesse." *German Life and
    Letters,* VI (1952–1953), 117–127.
Artiss, David. "Key Symbols in Hesse's *Steppenwolf." Seminar,* VII
    (1971), 85–101.
Bandy, Stephen C. "Herman Hesse's *Das Glasperlenspiel* in Search of
    Josef Knecht." *Modern Language Quarterly,* XXXIII (1972),
    299–311.
Boulby, Mark. *Hermann Hesse: His Mind and Art.* Ithaca: Cornell
    University Press, 1967.
Colby, Thomas E. "The Impenitent Prodigal: Hermann Hesse's Hero."
    German Quarterly, XL (1967), 14–23.
Derrenberger, John. "Who Is Leo? Astrology in Hermann Hesse's *Die
    Morgenlandfahrt." Monatshefte,* LXVII (1975), 167–172.
Dhority, Lynn. "Who Wrote the *Tractat von Steppenwolf?" German
    Life and Letters,* XXVII (1973/1974), 59–66.
Engel, Eva J. "Hermann Hesse." *German Men of Letters,* II. London:
    Wolff, 1963, 249–274.
Fickert, Kurt. "The Development of the Outsider Concept in Hesse's
    Novels." *Monatshefte,* LII (1960), 171–178.
Field, G. W. *Hermann Hesse.* New York: Twayne Publishers, 1970.
———. "Hermann Hesse as Critic of English and American Litera-
    ture." *Monatshefte,* LIII (1961), 147–158.
———. "Music and Morality in Thomas Mann and Hermann Hesse."
    University of Toronto Quarterly, XXIV (1955), 175–190.
Flaxman, Seymour. *"Der Steppenwolf:* Hesse's Portrait of the Intellec-
    tual." *Modern Language Quarterly,* XL (1954), 346–358.
Freedman, Ralph. *The Lyrical Novel: Studies in Hermann Hesse, Andre
    Gide and Virginia Woolf.* Princeton: Princeton University Press,
    1963.
———. "Romantic Imagination: Hermann Hesse as a Modern Novel-
    ist." *Publications of the Modern Language Association of America,*
    LXXIII (1958), 275–284.
Heller, Peter. "The Creative Unconscious and the Spirit: A Study of
    Polarities in Hesse's Image of the Writer." *Modern Language
    Forum,* XXXVIII (1958), 28–40.
———. "The Writer in Conflict with His Age: A Study in the Ideology
    of Hermann Hesse." *Monatshefte,* XLVI (1954), 137–147.

Hill, Claude. "Hermann Hesse and Germany." *German Quarterly,* XXI (1948), 9–15.

Johnson, Sidney M. "The Autobiographies in Hermann Hesse's *Glasperlenspiel.*" *German Quarterly,* XXIX (1956), 160–171.

Koch, Stephen. "Prophet of Youth. Hermann Hesse's *Narcissus and Goldmund.*" *The New Republic* (July 13, 1968), 23–26.

Koester, Rudolf. "The Portrayal of Age in Hesse's Narrative Prose." *Germanic Review,* XLI (1966), 11–19.

————. "Self-Realization: Hesse's Reflections on Youth." *Monatshefte,* LVII (1965), 181–186.

————. "Terminal Sanctity or Benign Banality. The Critical Controversy Surrounding Hermann Hesse." *Bulletin of the Rocky Mountain Language Association,* XXVII (1973), 59–63.

Maurer, Warren R. "Jean Paul and Hermann Hesse: *Katzenberger* and *Kurgast.*" *Seminar,* LV (1968), 113–128.

Middleton, J. C. "An Enigma Transfigured in Hermann Hesse's *Glasperlenspiel.*" *German Life and Letters,* X (1956–1957), 298–302.

————. "Hermann Hesse's *Morgenlandfahrt.*" *Germanic Review,* XXXII (1957), 299–310.

Mileck, Joseph. *"Das Glasperlenspiel.* Genesis, Manuscripts and Publication." *German Quarterly,* XLIII (1970), 299–310.

————. *Hermann Hesse and His Critics.* Chapel Hill: University of North Carolina Press. 1958.

————. "Names and the Creative Process." *Monatshefte,* LIII (1961), 167–180.

————. "The Poetry of Hermann Hesse." *Monatshefte,* LXVI (1954), 192–198.

————. "The Prose of Hermann Hesse: Life, Substance, Form." *German Quarterly,* XXVII (1954), 163–174.

Naumann, Walter. "The Individual and Society in the Work of Hermann Hesse." *Monatshefte,* XLI (1949), 33–42.

Negus, Kenneth. "On the Death of Joseph Knecht in Hermann Hesse's *Glasperlenspiel.*" *Monatshefte,* LIII (1961), 181–189.

Norton, Roger C. *Hermann Hesse's Futuristic Idealism.* The Glass Bead Game *and Its Predecessors.* Bern: H. Long, 1973.

Otten, Anna. *Hesse Companion.* Frankfurt-am-Main: Suhrkamp. 1970.

Paslick, Robert H. "Dialectic and Non-Attachment: The Structure of Hermann Hesse's *Siddhartha.*" *Symposium,* XXVII (1973), 64–75.

Peppard, Murray B. "Hermann Hesse: From Eastern Journey to Castalia." *Monatshefte,* L (1958), 247–256.

————. "Hermann Hesse's Ladder of Learning." *Kentucky Foreign Language Quarterly,* III (1956), 13–20.

————. "Notes on Hesse's Narrative Technique." *Kentucky Foreign Language Quarterly,* VI (1959), 169–178.

Rose, Ernst. *Faith from the Abyss. Hermann Hesse's Way from Romanticism to Modernity.* New York: New York University Press, 1965.

Seidlin, Oskar. "Hermann Hesse's *Glasperlenspiel.*" *Germanic Review,* XXIII (1948), 263–273.

————. "Hermann Hesse. The Exorcism of the Demon." *Symposium,* IV (1950), 325–348.

Shaw, Leroy. "Time and the Structure of Hermann Hesse's *Siddhartha.*" *Symposium,* XI (1957), 204–224.

Sorell, Walter. *The Man Who Sought and Found Himself.* London: Wolff, 1974.

Timpe, Eugene. "Hermann Hesse in the United States." *Symposium,* XXIII (1969), 73–78.

Willson, A. Leslie. "Hesse's Veil of Isis." *Monatshefte,* LV (1963), 313–321.

Zeller, Bernhard. *Portrait of Hesse.* New York: Herder and Herder, 1971.

Ziolkowski, Theodore, ed. *Hesse. A Collection of Critical Essays.* Englewood Cliffs, N.J.: Prentice-Hall, 1973.

————. "Hermann Hesse: *Der vierte Lebenslauf.*" *Germanic Review,* XLII (1967), 124–143.

————. "Hermann Hesse's Chiliastic Vision." *Monatshefte,* LIII (1961), 199–210.

————. "Hermann Hesse's *Steppenwolf:* A Sonata in Prose." *Modern Language Quarterly,* XIX (1958), 115–133.

————. "Saint Hesse among the Hippies." *American-German Review,* XXXV (1969), 19–23.

————. *The Novels of Hermann Hesse: A Study in Theme and Structure.* Princeton: Princeton University Press, 1965.

————. "The Quest for the Grail in Hesse's *Demian.*" *Germanic Review,* XLIX (1974), 44–59.

49810005

Catalog

If you are interested in a list of fine Paperback
books, covering a wide range of subjects
and interests, send your name and address,
requesting your free catalog, to:

McGraw-Hill Paperbacks
1221 Avenue of Americas
New York, N.Y. 10020